MOBSTERS & RUMRUNNERS
of CANADA

—◆— Crossing the Line —◆—

GORD STEINKE

FOLK
LORE
PUBLISHING

The Publisher: Folklore Publishing
Website: www.folklorepublishing.com

National Library of Canada Cataloguing in Publication

Steinke, Gord
    Mobsters & rumrunners of Canada: crossing the line / by Gord Steinke.

(Legends series)
American ed. published under title: Crossing the line.
Includes bibliographical references.

ISBN-13: 978-1-894864-11-4
ISBN-10: 1-894864-11-5

    1. Smuggling—Canada—History—20th century. 2. Organized crime—United States—History—20th century. 3. Smugglers—Canada—History—20th century. 4. Prohibition—United States—History—20th century. 5. Prohibition—Canada—History—20th century. I. Steinke, Gord. Crossing the line. II. Title. III. Title: Mobsters and rumrunners of Canada. IV. Series: Legends series (Edmonton, Alta.)

HV5091.C3S727 2004   364.1'33   C2004-901751-9

Project Director: Faye Boer
Cover Image: Courtesy of The Library of Congress, USZ62-95475

Photography credits: Every effort has been made to accurately credit the sources of photographs. Any errors or omissions should be directed to the publisher for changes in future editions. *Photographs courtesy of* Archives of Ontario (p.91, RG-23-26-93-1.9); British Columbia Archives (p. 166, D-01777); Bill Guilfoyle (p. 70); Chicago Historical Society (p. 10, IChi-26183); Glenbow Archives, Calgary, Canada (p. 19, NA-2946-1; p. 185, NA-3282-1; p. 188, NA-3282-2; p. 197, NA-3537-1); Library of Congress (title page, USZ62-95475; p. 25, USZ62-97941; p. 38, USZ62-124966; p. 43, USZ62-108387; p. 56, USZ62-83079; p.58, USZ62-124983; p. 80, USZ62-12142; p. 98, USZ62-96027; p.116, USZ62-12143; p. 149, USZ62-96028; p. 160, USZ62-96152); Legal Archives Society of Alberta (p. 201); Moose Jaw Public Library (p.31); National Library of Canada (p. 105, NL-15185); The Mariners' Museum (p.141); Tunnels of Moose Jaw (p. 29); U.S. Coast Guard (p. 118; p. 123); Walter P. Reuther Library, Wayne State University (p. 87).

We acknowledge the support of the Alberta Foundation for the Arts for our publishing program.

PC:P5

Contents

ACKNOWLEDGMENTS

I am indebted to the following people who shared their family stories with me about rumrunners in Canada and the United States and to all those who helped me gather research for this book.

Hester Burton
Norm Hennigar
Earle Burgess
Bill Guilfoyle
RCMP Cst. Doug Winkleman
Glen Yearley
Bill Sass (Edmonton Journal)

Royal BC Museum
Powell River Historical Museum
Glenbow Alberta Archives
Crowsnest Pass Museum
Moose Jaw Tunnel Tour
Penumbra Publishing

DEDICATION

To all the families who lost loved ones on both sides of the law during the rum-running years in Canada. And to my wife Deb for all her encouragement and support.

Introduction

"Our country has deliberately undertaken a great
social and economic experiment, noble in motive
and far-reaching in purpose."

–Herbert Hoover, U.S. President on the 18th
Amendment enacting Alcohol Prohibition, 1919

PROHIBITION WAS A MISERABLE FAILURE. The so-called "Noble
Experiment," which was meant to reduce crime and poverty
and improve people's health instead ushered in an era of mayhem and murder that hasn't been rivaled since. When the clock
struck midnight on January 16, 1920, and America went dry,
mob-controlled liquor created a black-market business in
Canada and the U.S. For the next 13 years, Americans couldn't
even enjoy a glass of wine with dinner in their own homes
without breaking the law.

"The Noble Experiment" was in reality 13 years of greed and
bloodshed. Mobsters turned Prohibition into a multi-million
dollar underground industry. The 1920s saw a rapid increase in
the American crime rate, mainly because of the illegal liquor
trade that mob bosses created to serve their thirsty customers,
especially in large cities such as Chicago.

Rumrunners and bootleggers north of the border were eager to supply American mobsters with high-quality Canadian booze. The Soo Railroad line ran north from Chicago to Moose Jaw, creating the perfect opportunity for smugglers to transport Canadian liquor into the United States. Moose Jaw became known as "Little Chicago," and rumor had it that mobster Al Capone occasionally visited the prairie town to check up on his smuggling operations. A network of underground tunnels still exists in that prairie city that you can explore to this day.

When public pressure forced the U.S. government to repeal Prohibition in 1933, President Franklin D. Roosevelt remarked: "I think this would be a good time for a beer."

When I began researching this book on the Canadian connection to the American underworld during Prohibition, I had no idea it would take me on such a fascinating, colorful and often violent journey into a part of our country's history you don't often read or hear about. I was suspicious of the stories I'd heard over the years from hotel and bar owners, friends and family about the exploits of gangsters and rumrunners in Canada during the Roaring Twenties and early Thirties. They sounded more like tall tales than credible and factual accounts of Canadian history.

When you think about it, do you really believe that notorious mob boss Al Capone ever visited Moose Jaw, Saskatchewan? Unlikely. Or that Dutch Schultz, the cold-blooded killer from the Bronx did business with Canadian booze barons, the Bronfmans, in Bienfait, Saskatchewan? Preposterous! What are the odds, realistically, that a handful of decorated Canadian WWI naval officers would turn to a life of crime on the high seas and become pirates, smuggling thousands of gallons of Canadian whiskey to American mobsters. Impossible, you say? Don't be so quick to judge.

Mobsters and smugglers and their greedy lives filled with murder, mystery and mayhem are more often seen as a product of imaginative Hollywood screen writers and authors of pulp fiction, than a credible part of our country's history as taught in our Canadian schools. I interviewed people from BC to Nova Scotia about mobsters and rumrunners in Canada during this period, and it seemed that just about everyone had a story to share. I found it surprising that some people still feel a little guilty when talking about their family association with bootleggers and gangsters—even though it's 80 years after Prohibition! Others are proud of their family stories and the colorful role a great grandfather, uncle or aunt played during the rumrunning years.

Sometimes it was difficult to distinguish fact from fiction. I learned that the memory can sometimes become hazy when stories are passed along verbally over nearly a century. Other times, while gathering research, I found discrepancies in dates, places or even the spellings of names, and these had to be sorted out and corrected. Nonetheless, using a variety of newspaper articles, government archives and other publications, one undeniable common denominator emerged from our country's past—the cruel and greedy era of *Mobsters and Rumrunners of Canada* is a very real and important part of our Canadian heritage.

Some of the dialogue in this book is fictionalized to enhance reader enjoyment.

CHAPTER ONE

The Capone Connection

"Public service is my motto."

–Al Capone

SOUTHERN SASKATCHEWAN MUST HAVE SEEMED a million miles away to the shadowy figure standing alone on the platform at the Northwestern Train Station in Chicago on June 26, 1926. The stocky man in the beige fedora reached into the breast pocket of his camel hair top coat and pulled out a pack of Lucky Strikes. He looked around nervously to see if anyone noticed him. No one seemed to pay him any attention. It had been many years since he'd been on a train, and the acrid smell of burning diesel brought back memories of watching the trains at Brooklyn Station in New York City when he was a boy.

The day was overcast, cool and windy, but the platform was a bustle of activity as the passengers and railway workers went about their business. What the people didn't know was that the lonely figure who'd bought his ticket under the name Alphonse Raiola (Raiola was his mother's maiden name) was one of the most feared gangsters in North America. They had no idea that this unassuming man was the most dangerous and powerful man in America—"The Big Fellow" also known as "Scarface." It was Al Capone.

Capone's mob dynasty infiltrated all aspects of society. He ruled not only the Chicago underworld, but also law and order and public opinion. He bribed judges, politicians and the police for control of the city's bootlegging, gambling and prostitution. One of the most powerful men on his payroll at the time was the mayor of Chicago, William "Big Bill" Thompson. But in 1926, Thompson was up for re-election, and he decided his affiliation with the celebrity gangster was bad for his image. A month before the beginning of Thompson's campaign, he arranged a secret meeting with Scarface at the prestigious Lexington Hotel in downtown Chicago.

"You know I appreciate everything you've done for me, Al," Thompson told the mob boss in the third-floor boardroom Capone used as an office, "but I'm up for re-election, and the press is having a field day with our business relationship."

"So forget about it," Capone said. "Who cares what those gossip mongers scribble in their rags?"

"Well, I think it's in both our best interests that I get re-elected, and I'm thinking that you should maybe duck out of town for a couple of weeks until the election is over."

Thompson waited for Capone to explode in anger, but was surprised by the thoughtful look that came over the crime lord's wide face.

"You have a point, Billy," Capone said standing up. "I need you back in office. And maybe it's time I laid low for a while. Good idea. I'll plan to take a little trip."

And so Capone decided to take a working vacation. During Prohibition his mob organization had expanded north into Canada, where liquor still flowed freely. Prohibition had ended in Saskatchewan in 1924, and the time was right for Capone to check up on his Canadian connections and strengthen his ties with the Saskatchewan bootleggers. He was headed to the western nerve center of the Mafia's rum-running operation north of the border in Moose Jaw. Along the way he would also stop in

Public Enemy Number One. Al Capone, alias Scarface, (1899–1947) is one of the most recognizable gangsters in history. He ran Chicago with blood and guns.

the Saskatchewan town of Bienfait where he had arranged a business meeting with Canadian entrepreneurs and brothers Sam and Harry Bronfman.

Capone boarded the train as the conductor looked up and down the track under the train shed. It was 12:45 PM, and the old conductor had been on his feet since 5:00 AM. He was in no mood for stragglers. He wanted to get the last of the passengers and their luggage on *The Mountaineer* #998. The massive steam engine built in Pittsburgh in 1917 was one of the first trains with all-steel cars, replacing the more treacherous wooden ones. This particular train only made the Chicago–Vancouver CPR Soo Line run during the warm summer months.

Despite the train's stained-glass ceiling windows and floral designs in dark mahogany wall panels, Capone was unimpressed. He'd paid the extra $2.80 for the executive sleeper with a private shower because he wanted his privacy, but he was a man of style and accustomed to luxury. He would have to make do with the Spartan conditions while attending to business in Saskatchewan. His Prohibition customers were always demanding more product, and his mission was to get the liquor supply flowing faster across the border to his many thirsty customers.

Prohibition had been introduced as "The Noble Experiment," and 33 states were in the middle of a dry spell. It was the Roaring Twenties, a time of great social change that heralded a sense of optimism and excitement now that the Great War was over. As F. Scott Fitzgerald wrote, "The parties were bigger, the pace was faster, the shows were broader, the buildings were higher, the morals were looser and the liquor was cheaper." It was a time of new innovations—the Model T Ford, radios, dishwashers, electric toasters and refrigerators. The Jazz Age had begun; skirts were above the knee. It was a time for heroes, like Charles Lindburgh, Babe Ruth and Jack Dempsey. The Roaring Twenties set the tone for the rest of the century.

Capone shut the door to his tiny berth, hung his hat on the back of the door and eased himself onto the lower bunk. He pulled out his watch; he had time to kill. In Eau Claire, Wisconsin, 310 miles up the track, some of his associates would join him.

He settled back and drifted off to sleep, waking with a start sometime later. He felt uneasy. The 8' by 5' compartment gave him nightmares about being in a prison cell. For a brief moment, caught between nightmare and waking, he felt disoriented. His first thoughts were of his wife Mae and his seven-year-old son, Sonny. He was deeply devoted to his Irish-born wife, Mary "Mae" Coughlin, who turned heads with her striking beauty.

He'd met the quiet, glamorous blonde at a dance in Brooklyn in 1917. The couple had a son on December 4, 1918, and named him Albert "Sonny" Francis. Capone and Mae were married 26 days later. It was true love. Mae loved her bad boy gangster, and she stuck by Capone throughout all his affairs, brushes with the law, execution attempts and prison time.

Capone was born on January 17, 1899, in Brooklyn, New York. He grew up in a tough neighborhood and earned a reputation as a ruthless street fighter in several teenage gangs. Although he was highly intelligent, and education came easy to him, Capone quit school in grade six. A few years later, at the tender age of 14, he went to work for mob boss Frankie Yale.

When he was 17, Capone received his infamous facial scars and the nickname "Scarface" in a bar fight after insulting the sister of another gangster, Frank Gallucio. He also proved his willingness to kill early on, murdering two men while a member of Yale's notorious Five Points Gang. New York Police called the gang "a farm club for the Mafia." It was in this gang that Capone (and others, such as Lucky Luciano) learned to fight with knives and use revolvers. Capone was never convicted of the murders, but Frankie Yale sent him to Chicago until things cooled off. Capone arrived in the Windy City in 1919. By the end of that year 33 states had gone dry.

Meanwhile, in Canada, temperance movements were gaining momentum, preaching about the evils of alcohol. In 1918, the Canadian government closed all distilleries and breweries as part of the War Measures Act. It didn't seem right that Canadians were partying and enjoying a drink while so many young men were dying on the battlefields in Europe. Grain was needed for food production, as a result, distilleries could manufacture only industrial and medicinal alcohol to aid the war effort. But the laws only lasted two years, and in 1918 when the boys came marching home, federal Prohibition ended in Canada.

At that time, individual provinces were given the option to control the manufacture and sale of alcohol. Although some provinces did experiment with some form of Prohibition, the laws did not become widespread. Prohibition in Canada was a farce; all the loopholes were exploited. But it was a much different picture in the United States.

American leaders were determined to make Prohibition work south of the 49th parallel. On January 16, 1920, at midnight, one of the most popular recreational pastimes suddenly came to a grinding halt in the U.S. With the 18th Amendment, all importing, exporting, manufacturing and selling of liquor stopped in order to reduce the consumption of alcohol, and theoretically, reduce crime, poverty and death rates, while improving the economy and quality of life.

Soon after the law went into effect a free-for-all erupted among opportunistic criminals, and a powder keg of corruption ignited among the police, judges and politicians. Organized crime, bootlegging, union tampering and the sex trade spread like viruses. Saloons—and there were many of them—went underground and became speakeasies that needed bootleg booze in a hurry. The competition for territory turned violent, and by the end of Prohibition, at least 800 gangsters had been killed in bootleg-related shootings in Chicago.

"When I sell liquor, it's bootlegging. When my patrons serve it on a silver tray on Lakeshore Drive, it's hospitality," Al Capone once said.

To get the booze flowing, the Mafia looked north for its supply. Canada was far from dry. Prohibition had ended in Saskatchewan in 1924, and liquor was being distributed legally from province to province. For example, in Yorkton, Saskatchewan, brothers Sam and Harry Bronfman created the Canada Pure Drug Company so they could legally manufacture and distribute "medicinal" alcohol. So it wasn't long before the Mafia set their sights on their enterprising neighbors to the north and came up with clever ways to smuggle the alcohol into the U.S.

Between 1925 and 1932, Capone controlled all the distilleries, nightclubs, bookie joints, gambling houses, brothels and race tracks in the Chicago area at a reported income of over $100 million per year. It's said that in one year, Al Capone made $60 million (the equivalent of about $2 billion today) in liquor sales. One can only imagine the huge amounts of payola being quietly slipped into the pockets of politicians, judges and police. But even though his business was booming in Chicago, Capone wanted more.

The Chicago mob boss went to his private room in the sleeper car to get away from the constant chatter of the other passengers and the kids running up and down the aisle. His neck was sore. He'd only been on the train for four hours, and already the constant clickety-clack of steel wheels on rails was giving him a headache. Maybe he should have had one of his bodyguards drive him to Canada. But the thought of 300 FBI agents combing the highways and back roads trying to track him down quickly reminded him the train was the most inconspicuous way to travel.

He crawled out of his tiny bed on the train, careful not to bang his head, and sat on the padded bench in front of the window watching the Wisconsin farmland rush by. He was thirsty, so he walked out into the narrow corridor. Outside the public gentleman's washroom was a water cooler. He grabbed a paper cup and poured an ice-cold drink.

Capone pulled out his watch; it was just after 5:00 PM. His bodyguards would be boarding at the Eau Claire station in about an hour and a half to join him for the rest of the trip. So far, it seemed that he'd slipped out of Chicago without being noticed. That made him breathe a little easier, and he began to relax.

The smell of food cooking reminded him that he hadn't eaten since breakfast, so he went back to his room, put on his hat and strolled down to the dining car.

It was well known that *The Mountaineer* hired some of the best chefs for its summer runs. It was also no secret that Capone was a man who enjoyed a good meal. He poked his head in the cook's galley.

"Hey there, how's the food on this trip?" Capone asked the startled chef.

"It's always top notch sir, " the cook answered, not recognizing the Chicago gangster.

Capone flipped him a silver dollar.

"Here, make sure I get a healthy portion. The big guy is hungry," grinned Capone. He strolled into the dining room and sat down at a table with a mother and her teenage daughter.

"What looks good tonight?" asked Capone, as he picked up the menu.

"I'm having the Swiss steak," the girl replied.

"Shush, girl, don't talk to strangers," her mother said, nudging her daughter gently.

"That's right, missy. Listen to your mother." Capone leaned forward. The girl could smell his expensive cologne and tobacco. "You never know what sort of unsavory types you'll meet on a train."

Capone gave her a sly wink and then ordered the three of them Swiss steak with all the trimmings.

When Capone had finished eating, he stood up to leave. From habit he took out a $20 bill to leave as a tip. Realizing that the exorbitant gratuity would simply draw attention, he quickly stuffed the bill back in his jacket pocket and instead placed a silver dollar in the saucer. He returned to the passenger car to await his colleagues who were boarding at the Eau Claire station.

He was looking forward to seeing his old buddies and long-time bodyguards Tony and Jack. The two triggermen were deadly. Over the years they'd laughed and killed together and had been through several mob wars. Tony and Jack respected and feared Capone.

Tony "Joe Batters" Accardo was the main triggerman for the Syndicate. He was a stocky, powerful man with black hair, hooded eyes and a nose that looked like it had been punched one too many times. He got his nickname after he smashed the skulls of two Capone rivals with a baseball bat. Capone was impressed and said, "This boy is a real Joe Batters." Born in Chicago's Little Sicily in 1906, he was already a veteran of the Syndicate by age 20, having been a career criminal since he was 15. He'd been arrested 27 times but bragged that he'd never spent a night in jail. Tony was also a deeply religious man who never went anywhere without a miniature bible in his breast pocket. He was known to quote scripture at the strangest times, especially after he'd just committed murder.

Joe Batters officially became a "made" man in the Chicago Mob a month before he was hired to accompany Capone to Saskatchewan. A "made man" is a gang member who has moved up the mob ladder by proving his loyalty to the gang. They are usually rewarded with a special task or territory. As a "made man" Batters had Capone's utmost respect; he was guaranteed full protection by the mob and bound by the mafia's code of silence. Capone promoted Batters to be one of his main bodyguards for his loyalty. He was often seen sitting in the lobby of Capone's headquarters, The Lexington Hotel, with a machine gun in his lap. But police didn't bother him because Capone owned most of Chicago's judges and police at the time.

"Machine Gun" Jack McGurn was born in 1905 and raised in Chicago's Little Italy. He got his nickname from his weapon of choice—a rapid-fire tommy gun. During his career, Jack was credited with more than 25 kills for the Capone Mob. A handsome man with jet black hair, slicked back and parted down the middle, he always wore expensive three-piece black suits with a gold pocket watch—a cold-blooded killer with a sense of style.

McGurn was Capone's favorite hit man, and he was frequently seen at his boss's side watching Babe Ruth in action and at other social events. A caricature of the Jazz Age, he strummed a ukulele, dated some of Chicago's most glamorous chorus girls and fancied himself a homegrown version of Rudolph Valentino. It's believed that McGurn was the mastermind behind the St. Valentine's Day Massacre on February 14, 1929.

Jack and Tony were anxious. They weren't really sure what the Boss had in store for them in Saskatchewan. They'd been partying at Capone's fortress hideaway in Couderay, Wisconsin, laying low and waiting for their orders. They passed the time golfing, fishing, drinking whiskey and entertaining girls driven in from St. Paul, Minnesota.

They'd driven down to Eau Claire in the morning fighting hangovers. They were trying their best to look sharp and had slurped down a great deal of black coffee before the train pulled into the station.

"Hey mister, are these seats taken?"

Capone turned in his seat to see Jack and Tony standing in the aisle grinning. He'd been looking up and down the platform watching for his boys but hadn't seen them.

"You snuck up on me! Sit down."

Both men carried army duffel bags and a suitcase. After stowing their gear in the overhead rack, they hung their coats on the hook by the window and sat down.

"Any trouble?" asked Joe.

"Nope. All quiet so far."

For the next hour, as the train rolled towards Portal, Saskatchewan, the three men spoke in hushed tones as Capone explained the details of their Canadian trip. After a stopover in St. Paul, they'd carry on throughout the night until they arrived at North Portal and Canada Customs the following day. Capone told the two men that they would be making two stopovers during the next four weeks while they did business in Canada.

The first layover would be in a place called Bienfait, Saskatchewan, where liquor moguls Sam and Harry Bronfman were making a fortune in the booze business. From 1917 to 1924, Saskatchewan had been dry. But when Prohibition was repealed by popular vote, the Bronfmans turned to an even larger market, the United States. Since Prohibition wouldn't end in the U.S. until 1933, Sam and Harry took full advantage of the situation. At the time, it was perfectly legal to distribute alcohol from province to province using the CPR line. But it wasn't legal to smuggle liquor by the hundreds of gallons into the U.S., where Prohibition was in full force. That didn't stop Harry and Sam. It is said that the brothers' family business would never have become the multi-billion dollar Seagram's empire if it hadn't been for the huge demand for booze from south of the border during the 1920s.

Harry and Sam made whiskey at their distillery in Yorkton, Saskatchewan, and sold it to a wide variety of American gangsters including Al Capone in Chicago, Lucky Luciano in New York and the Purple Gang in Detroit. These gangs would then send their "boys" north to Canada to smuggle it across the border in order to sell it to their Prohibition-thirsty customers.

The gangsters were creative at coming up with clever ways to fool the customs officials. They'd hide the liquor in false gas tanks in Model Ts, fill tire tubes with whiskey and air, hide

Last chance sale. A mail-order liquor price list from the Yorkton Distributing Company before Prohibition was enacted in Saskatchewan in 1915 large caches of booze in granaries, wells and under stacks of straw and sometimes they'd even carry the liquor across the border on foot or horseback.

But smuggling booze into the U.S. was risky. Dealing with gangsters was bad for your health and could shorten your life span, not to mention that life behind bars wasn't exactly an attractive option. But the lure of easy money outweighed the risks, and the Bronfmans were shrewd businessmen. They made sure that profits were high and that the mob took most of the risks when they dealt with cold-blooded killers like Al Capone.

Capone's second stop would be in Moose Jaw, 150 miles farther west along the line. Capone had been running liquor successfully out of that prairie city into Minneapolis since Prohibition ended on the prairies in 1924, but he thought that he could squeeze more out of his distributors. The complex series of underground tunnels that connected most of Moose Jaw's 23 hotels made it an ideal location to conduct business without ever being seen.

Capone had a man overseeing his operation there; Diamond Jim Grady had been running the bootlegging operation for the past few years. Diamond Jim was a familiar sight around Moose Jaw, standing a lanky 6'4" and easily recognizable because he had diamonds set into his front teeth.

As *The Mountaineer* chugged towards Canada, Capone and his men talked about the operation in hushed tones in Capone's cabin.

"I don't see any trouble from these Canadians," Capone said, lighting up a fat Cuban cigar, "but if they try to back out or double-cross us, that's where you step in. Did you bring Tommy?"

"We both brought Tommy," said McGurn.

The hired guns were talking about the Thompson submachine guns they had packed away in their duffel bags. A highly effective killing machine, the tommy gun was the weapon of choice for the city gangsters because of its accuracy at close range. It featured all-steel, high quality construction with partially ribbed barrels for better cooling. It weighed 11 pounds and could fire 700 .45 mm rounds per minute. Because the barrel was just 267 mm, and it had a detachable buttstock, it was easy to hide in a suitcase.

The Mountaineer #998 was nearing Estevan, Saskatchewan. Capone was eager to get off the train and check into the White Hotel in Bienfait. He'd been traveling for more than 16 hours, and the landscape of flat prairie dotted with grain elevators and lined with barbed wire fences was beginning to get to him. He wanted a hot shower, a good meal and a bed that he could stretch out on. The train pulled into Estevan. Capone, McGurn and Accardo stepped onto the platform into a beautiful sunny prairie day. They were met by American, Arthur S. Flegenheimer (alias Dutch Schultz).

Dutch was a loyal soldier who had been on Capone's payroll for five years. He'd been coming to Saskatchewan occasionally since 1922 to make sure Capone's whiskey smuggling operation was running smoothly. By now he had an entire smuggling scenario worked out. Hiring teenage boys for 50 cents a day to do the actual smuggling, he knew all the tricks of the trade and taught his boys well. From 4:00 to 6:00 PM on weekdays, the boys would load the cars and then drive the booze to a south Saskatchewan border crossing into the waiting arms of American rumrunners. The boys were his safest bet for the job.

"Who's gonna stop a kid?" he was often heard to say.

One clever ploy that had proved successful over the years was to use two identical Buicks, one driven by one of his boys and the other by an American smuggler. When they got to the border, they didn't bother to transfer the liquor from one car to another; they just switched license plates. He also told the teenagers not to drive over 35 miles per hour to avoid raising the Mounties' suspicion.

Another "quick-change" ploy also involved using identical cars. One car was in the garage of a home, and the other could be camouflaged in a stand of trees. If the driver suspected the police were about to nab him, he could drive the loaded car into the trees and then quickly walk to his house, meeting the police so that they could check the clean car in the garage. It was a well-honed system.

Dutch Schultz was a man you didn't want to cross. He had a violent temper; he enjoyed a fight, whether it be with guns or fists; and he had a deep hatred for authority.

Schultz arrived at the Estevan station in a green 1923 Model T Ford. The four men loaded up their gear and drove east to Bienfait. By 9:00 PM they were checked into their rooms on the second floor of the White Hotel on Railroad Avenue. They went down to the pub to enjoy a bottle or two of good Canadian whiskey and play pool.

The tiny prairie town was booming. Coal mining in the area provided a good living to hundreds of miners and their families. It had all the amenities that life in a 1920s Saskatchewan town could offer. The town had grown so quickly since the first general store was built in 1905. In 1926, the town had a bank, a post office, a church, a school, a pool hall, a barbershop, a hardware store and a livery and feed barn. Main Street even boasted a movie theatre with movies shown on a projector that was cranked by hand and a dance-hall with entertainment every Saturday night provided by a local band, the Night Hawks. The five-piece group played all the top ragtime and jazz tunes of the day.

But behind the quiet façade lurked a sinister underworld. Not only was Bienfait home to part of the Bronfman liquor empire, it was becoming a stopover for ruthless American gangsters looking to cut a deal with the liquor moguls.

One of the first deals the Bronfmans made was with Al Capone's New York counterpart and close friend, Lucky Luciano. Capone and Lucky had known each other since grade school in New York.

Luciano had recently said to Capone, "Sam Bronfman was bootleggin' enough whiskey across the Canadian border to double the size of Lake Erie." Capone wanted to strike a similar deal for his Chicago operation.

Smuggling booze across the U.S. border was highly risky. If a smuggler was caught by one of the many roving police patrols, the resulting fines, jail time and the confiscation of the goods could wipe out profits and spoil a lucrative business opportunity. But money talks, and the smugglers were willing to take the risk. The successful ones stayed one step ahead of the law by frequently changing their smuggling methods in order to confuse the police.

Sam Bronfman met Capone, Schultz, McGurn and Accardo in the White Hotel lobby the afternoon after the three arrived.

"Nice to meet you, gentlemen, "Sam said, extending his hand. "This is my brother Harry. Welcome to Saskatchewan, home of the best whiskey this side of the St. Lawrence."

Capone shook Sam's hand. The steely-eyed gazes of the other gangsters sent a chill down Sam's back. He wondered if he'd made a mistake cutting a deal with these hardened criminals.

Sam and Harry drove the gangsters out to one of their three Boozoriums south of town. Capone couldn't believe his eyes. Here, in the middle of nowhere, 1000 miles from Chicago, was a warehouse filled with hundreds of barrels of whiskey.

For three days, Capone and Bronfman talked business. Sam promised he could deliver as many cases of whiskey as Capone wanted to buy. Capone agreed to purchase the highly prized Canadian whiskey. Twenty-four four-quart bottles of booze were packed in burlap sacks stuffed with straw and then packed in barrels. Each barrel cost the Bronfmans $24 to make, and

Sam sold a barrel to Al Capone for $140. Capone bought a car-load of 14 barrels and agreed to buy a similar amount weekly.

An instant bond forged between the two men. They had similar rags-to-riches stories, and both were feared for their violent tempers. Each came from dirt-poor immigrant families. Capone's mother and father came from Italy to the United States, and in 1889 Bronfman's parents had fled Russia, where making whiskey was a way of life. The name "Bronfman" literally means "whiskey man" in Yiddish, and so the brothers simply continued the cultural and family tradition.

Bronfman and his brothers had started from scratch in Yorkton, Saskatchewan, making whiskey in a warehouse. They were soon making a healthy profit selling liquor across Canada. But their business really boomed when they began selling whiskey to American bootleggers during Prohibition in the 1920s. The Bronfman empire was born and continues to flourish today under the Seagram's name.

It's not known exactly how much the Capone-Bronfman deal was worth, but by today's standards it was likely in the millions. The two formed a partnership and a friendship that lasted more than 10 years.

But illicit dealings inevitably come with violence. One incident that happened in the area four years earlier highlights the ruthlessness and lack of respect for human life that these 1920s pirates showed for anyone who got in their way. The brutal murder shocked the small prairie town and led to a frustrating series of dead ends for the RCMP.

On October 4, 1922, the body of Paul Matoff was found on a back road about two miles south of Bienfait. He'd been killed with a single shotgun blast to the chest. Matoff was the Bronfmans' brother-in-law and family business partner. It was Matoff who often conducted the business meetings with the mob and then arranged the booze exchange with the American gangsters. His murder was never solved, but the talk around

A Roaring Twenties "Flapper Girl" removes a flask of liquor from her Russian boot. It's believed that the term "bootleg" originated from the practice of concealing a flask in high-top boots. In the 1920s, a new woman was born. "The Flapper" smoked using a long cigarette holder, drank, danced and voted. She had short sleek hair, wore makeup and partied to crazy jazz all night long. A Flapper was a reckless rebel who embraced life and symbolized a sexy revolution in fashion. Bare arms were exposed while a tight corset ensured a chest as flat as a board. By 1921, the longer skirt was back—some long and uneven— the perfect cover-up while hiding liquor in her tall leather boots. She embodied the modern spirit of the Jazz Age.

town was that a Chicago gangster gunned him down over a booze deal gone bad.

But there was no violence when Capone and Bronfman shook hands and sealed their deal on that warm summer night in a field south of Bienfait. It looked more like a gentleman's agreement than a ruthless negotiation for an illegal operation that could put them both behind bars.

Capone could now run imported and locally distilled booze from the Boozorium in Saskatchewan to Minneapolis and then to his home base in Chicago using cars, trucks and the Soo line. The gangsters celebrated the new transaction with their Canadian hosts that night in the hotel bar, toasting their continued good health.

The next evening, Dutch drove the gangsters and their luggage back to the Estevan station. At midnight, they boarded the train and carried on west to Moose Jaw. Capone hoped to strike an even bigger booze-smuggling deal there in the booming prairie town with the help of his friend Diamond Jim Grady.

It was just after midnight, and the rail cars were dark as the weary passengers tried to sleep. As the dark, prairie towns rolled by—Milestone, Rouleau, Regina and Briar Crest—the three men said goodnight, settling in for some sleep on the final leg of their journey on the Soo Line through Saskatchewan on *The Mountaineer* #998.

"That son of a bitch better be there when we pull in."

Capone struggled to get his suitcase out of the luggage rack above his seat as *The Mountaineer* arrived at Moose Jaw station just as dawn was breaking on the morning of July 1. They'd been on the train for more than five hours, and Capone was sick and tired of being treated like a second-class citizen. While his fellow Americans were getting ready to celebrate July 4 as best they could without any legal booze, Tony and Jack were getting their gear out of the luggage racks and preparing to get off the train.

The "son of a bitch" Capone was referring to was Diamond Jim Grady, whose diamond smile shone in the bright prairie sun. Every two-bit huckster, moonshiner and five-and-dime hood knew he was a member of the Chicago mob, but they never really expected to see the big boss in town.

Grady was responsible for single-handedly running the bootlegging business in the Moose Jaw area. He made sure hundreds of gallons of booze made it to the train station via the underground tunnels and then on to the U.S. He'd had his run of the town for the past five years and walked around as if he owned the place, but even he never expected to see Al Capone.

Diamond Jim Grady used to be one of Capone's top triggermen in Chicago but got into some trouble with the boss when he started dating one of Capone's ex-girlfriends. When Al found out what was going on, he sent the pretty boy to the regions, as far north as the Syndicate's influence would take him. It was either that or risk torture (usually by a lit cigarette), a bullet in the stomach and to be left bleeding to death on some Illinois back road. Diamond Jim was flattered, but he was nervous and afraid now that Scarface was in town.

Diamond Jim was no lightweight gangster. He'd been accused of 11 murders, five in Canada from 1922 to 1924 and six in Chicago in 1919. Rumors circulated that he'd pistol-whipped a man to death in a bar fight in Minneapolis for cheating at cards. But it had been years since Diamond Jim had seen Al Capone face to face, and the man he watched step off the train looked nothing like the man he remembered.

This Al Capone looked like a vicious bulldog dressed in the height of fashion. He wore brown and cream patent leather shoes, and his coat was open with the collar up and his fedora pulled low. Jim could see a diamond and gold stickpin clasped to a yellow and green checked tie. The Big Fellow stepped lightly off the train and looked directly at Diamond Jim, who was standing on the platform. Two goons quickly stepped down behind Al and looked around at the wooden buildings and unpaved roads. They were a long way from home.

Before any formalities could be exchanged, Diamond Jim quickly ushered his visitors to the west side of the platform. An old Asian man and his teenage son were waiting for them. They grabbed the gangsters' bags and opened a door to what looked like an old coal chute. The six men stepped in and walked into a damp tunnel lined with pitted cement. The old wooden stairs were dimly lit by a single light bulb hanging from a frayed electrical cord. About 15 steps down, they stopped, and looking up from the dirt floor, they saw a long, dark brick-lined tunnel ahead.

"Welcome to The Jaw," said a nervous Diamond Jim with his best smile, as he stuck out his hand. "Nice to see you guys."

Tony and Jack could have cared less, but Al greeted him warmly. "I hear you're doing a great job here, Jim," Capone said, pumping his hand, "but I want you to do more. We need to double the whiskey coming out of here."

"We'll talk, Mr. Capone. Right now, follow me. These old Chinamen tunnels will take us to any hotel in town."

The Moose Jaw tunnels were built in the late 1800s by Chinese people who lived under the stores and hotels illegally. Many worked on the CPR. It was the time when many western Canadians were afraid of what was known as the "yellow peril." Ottawa had brought in restrictions on the number of Chinese immigrants that were allowed into the country so as not to take away too many jobs from Canadians. The government even imposed a head tax on every Chinese immigrant. Many of these workers were unable to afford the tax, so they went underground to hide from the authorities. Eventually, many of the immigrants smuggled in their wives and even raised families in the dark secret tunnels under Moose Jaw.

History comes alive in the Moose Jaw tunnel tour. Actors in period costumes take you on a journey back to a time when Moose Jaw was known as "Little Chicago." During the '20s, the Saskatchewan town became something of a gangsters' resort. Members of the Chicago mob, including Al Capone, visited the bustling town to sample the gambling and prostitution offered in the 23 hotels and also to check on their lucrative liquor-smuggling operations. The re-enactment show, which has become the city's most popular tourist attraction, comes complete with gangsters, tommy guns and barrels of stashed whiskey. The sounds of honky-tonk jazz filter through the dimly lit bar of Miss Fanny's brothel and speakeasy from an authentic player piano. The gangsters and molls lead you down into a maze of underground tunnels beneath the streets from where thousands of cases of bootleg booze were secreted to the train station and smuggled to the U.S.

However, by the 1920s, decades after the railroad was completed and the workers long gone, the tunnels took on an entirely different purpose. With Prohibition firmly enacted in the U.S., Moose Jaw became an American gangsters' haven. The Moose Jaw CPR station was a major stop along the Soo Line that linked Canada to the U.S., and it quickly became the perfect place for mobsters and rumrunners to smuggle alcohol onto the trains and ship it south of the border.

Jim warned the men to watch their heads as they made their way down the long, dark tunnel. They walked for a least a city block before they heard music and laughter.

"We're under the Royal Hotel; our stop is just under the street at the Brunswick," said Grady, as they walked. "How long ya in town for?" Diamond Jim had to duck his head to direct his question back at Capone.

"Long as it takes," was the only reply he got, as the tunnel took a sharp left, and they trudged through the dim light.

"We've got 23 hotels and nightclubs in town. We like to call The Jaw "Little Chicago." We'll have a good time."

The two triggermen looked at each other and rolled their eyes.

Once they were under Royal Street Jim stopped at an alcove and banged on a heavy wooden door. It swung open without a sound, and the four men climbed stairs that led them to a door in the Brunswick Hotel's kitchen. The hotel would be home for the next few days. Grady took his American visitors up the backstairs to their rooms. When Capone got to his door, he said he wanted to get cleaned up, take a nap and relax for the rest of the day.

The next morning, the Chicago mob boss got right to work. Grady met him at his room and took Capone down the backstairs, into the tunnels and to a meeting room in the basement of the Royal Hotel. The six Canadian thugs who ran the bootlegging operation for Diamond Jim rose out of respect when Capone entered the room. They were surprised by how short

"Little Chicago," as Moose Jaw, Saskatchewan was known when bootlegging, prostitution and gambling thrived in the prairie town during Prohibition

and pudgy the legendary gangster was. Nonetheless, they knew that they were in the company of a living legend and paid him the utmost respect.

"Welcome sir." A wiry Irishman stepped forward. "It's an honor to have you in our town. My name is Darcy, but they call me Shorty."

"Why don't you introduce the guys to Mr. Capone, Shorty?" Grady said, as he poured a couple of drinks. "Anything you need you just—"

Capone cut him off.

"Lookit. I'm not here on a pleasure trip. The reason I'm in Moose Jaw is simple," Capone told the Grady Gang. "I need you to double the amount of liquor you're sending stateside."

The awestruck hoods nodded in agreement. They knew that getting the many bootleggers in and around town to increase production was going to be an easy sell. In these tough times, they were more than willing to take Capone's money. The men shook hands, and the deal was done.

Grady and Capone headed back down into the tunnels. Next on the agenda was a meeting with Moose Jaw's chief of police, Walter Johnson. Capone was familiar with the chief's seedy reputation. The local gamblers, prostitutes and rum smugglers had a popular phrase when it came to the lawman: "Stay out of his way or prepare to pay." Capone was prepared to make the chief a wealthy man if he turned a blind eye to outgoing shipments.

Capone and Grady surfaced a few blocks to the northeast in the basement of the Empress Hotel. The two gangsters went up the backstairs to room 214 where Chief Johnson was waiting for them. In a friendly discussion, Capone assured Chief Johnson that his name would never be associated with the mob. He also told him that with the network of tunnels leading directly to the train yards, the local townsfolk would never see the liquor being loaded onto the trains. Chief Walter Johnson became a wealthy man that afternoon, and the men sealed the deal with a toast of whiskey from the chief's private stock.

Capone spent the next two days sick in his room with a sore throat and fever. He couldn't go to the local hospital, so Diamond Jim took him through the tunnels late one night to see a local doctor. Capone paid the man $250 in cash to remove his tonsils and to keep the entire affair quiet. According to the story, he even refused anesthetic.

While Capone lay recuperating in his hotel bed, his gunmen were whooping it up in the town's many saloons with their new-found Canadian buddies and the finest ladies of the evening that Saskatchewan had to offer. And although he was ill and only in Moose Jaw for a few days, Capone couldn't stay out of trouble. While his throat was healing, Diamond Jim Grady brought up a problem he was having with a small-time hood from Vancouver who was trying to muscle in on Jim's territory.

George Barradel, career criminal, had more brawn than brains. He and a few of his boys had been intruding on Grady's gambling parties in the tunnels, beating up clients and taking their money. Diamond Jim had already taken care of one of Barradel's thugs with a bullet to the head, but more kept coming. Capone decided to help out.

After hearing from a snitch that the rival gang was going to try another heist at an all-night gambling party at the Royal, Capone and Jack McGurn went to the speakeasy. (His other bodyguard, Tony Accardo, was missing in action. It seemed he'd gone on a drinking spree with a prostitute soon after arriving and hadn't been seen since.)

Jack sat at the table by the door reading the paper. Capone was slumped over a table in the back pretending to be passed out, his head on the table, a bottle of whiskey in front of him. A little after midnight, Barradel and five heavies crashed through the door.

"Your time's up Grady, you better pay up or else."

Without even looking up from his paper, Grady said, "Or else what? As far as I'm concerned, hell can freeze over, and I'm still not paying you one red cent."

One of the thugs reached over and ripped the paper out of Grady's hands. He slammed Diamond Jim's head onto the bar.

"Everyone out," he yelled. "This is between me and Grady."

One of the henchmen noticed the drunk passed out at the back table. He started walking over to Capone.

He was about five feet away when he said, "C'mon you old drunk. You heard me. Get outta here."

They were the last words that ever left his lips.

Capone suddenly sat up, pulled out the pair of .38s he had hidden under his coat and shot the startled gunman between the eyes. Before he even hit the floor, Jack stood up, pulled a tommy gun out from under the table and shot three more goons with two quick bursts. Capone walked up to the terrified hood who had been pounding Diamond Jim's head into the bar and shot him point blank in the face. Capone, Jack and Diamond Jim then walked calmly out the door and back into the tunnels.

For $100, Diamond Jim hired a group of Asians to clean up the mess and dispose of the bodies. It was a small price to pay considering he was never bothered again. Soon, his stable of bootleggers was brewing more booze than ever before, and he ran the successful Moose Jaw operation until Prohibition came to an end in the United States in 1933.

The following evening, a fierce summer rainstorm opened up on the southern prairies. A bloodhound tipped his head back and howled as the train left Moose Jaw station on the CPR Soo Line. Capone, McGurn and Accardo had quietly slipped out of town through the tunnels and boarded *The Mountaineer*. The three gangsters settled in for another long train ride, this time back to Chicago.

Capone was happy to be leaving what he considered hillbilly country in southern Saskatchewan. He yearned to be back in the big city with all the comforts it had to offer. He'd heard that Mayor William Thompson had been re-elected, and so he was clear to return home. But one thing was troubling him. Another gangster—Bugsy Malone—had started up a rival gang, which reportedly was hijacking some of Capone's booze shipments.

He leaned forward and whispered to McGurn, "You think Bugsy would have the balls to rip me off just cuz I'm out of town for a couple of weeks?"

"Kinda sounds that way boss." McGurn said.

"Not to worry," said Joe Batters, as he reached down and patted the duffel bag under his seat with the Thompson sub-machine gun hidden inside. "When we get to Chicago, we'll take care of business."

Satisfied with the answer, Capone slumped back in his seat and drifted off to sleep. They were going home.

By 1933, when Prohibition ended in the United States, the moonshine stills dried up in southern Saskatchewan and the bootleggers and rumrunners in Moose Jaw found themselves out of work. Diamond Jim went back to Chicago where he worked for many years as a trusted, faithful soldier in Capone's ruthless army. Eventually, the City of Moose Jaw boarded up and sealed off the maze of tunnels that ran under the city streets. The era of mobsters and rumrunners in the prairie town was over, but the legend of Al Capone and his Canadian connection lives on.

CHAPTER TWO

From the Bronx to Bienfait:
The Story of Dutch Schultz
(1902–1935)

*"He's a bit of a loon. He can go from zero
to psycho in seconds…"*

–Lucky Luciano

THE TOUGHEST TOUGH GUY OF ALL arrived in the tiny
Saskatchewan town of Bienfait in the summer of 1922. After
a long train ride from Chicago, Arthur Flegenheimer, alias
Dutch Schultz, stepped into the blazing prairie sun. The
20-year-old mobster was on a special mission at the request of
his boss, Al Capone: to set up a reliable liquor smuggling ring
with shipments into the U.S.

Schultz had on a well-worn grey suit, a buttoned-up shirt,
no necktie and a black fedora. He was a small man with jet
black hair, dark eyes and a nose that had seen the wrong side
of too many fistfights. A waitress who served him once in
Chicago said he looked a bit like Bing Crosby with his face
smashed in.

"Can I help you with your bags, sir?" asked a 12-year-old
kid standing among a group of friends watching the gangster
with curious interest.

"You sure can, boy," Dutch said. "Point me in the direction of the White Hotel. I need to get a room."

Arthur Flegenheimer was born in the Bronx on August 6, 1902. He was the son of a saloonkeeper, and his family lived in a tough neighborhood of New York City known as Jewish Harlem. Arthur grew up in a world of horse-drawn beer trucks, saloons, bartenders with striped shirts and sleeve garters, windup Victrolas, pool halls and Babe Ruth. Arthur went to Public School #12, the same facility where in 1932, the principal, Dr. John Condon, would toss $50,000 ransom money over the wall of St. Raymond's Cemetery in exchange for the Lindbergh baby.

Arthur was a well-behaved boy until he was 11, when his father deserted the family. After that he began getting into trouble. He hated school and was often strapped by the principal for skipping classes and getting into fights with other boys. He became cruel and sullen, horrifying his mother when he strangled Biscuit, the family dog, with his bare hands when he couldn't teach it to shake a paw.

He dropped out of school when he was 13 and went to work as an errand boy for a Bronx roofing company. But by the time he was 15, Arthur was hanging out with young toughs in neighborhood street gangs, stealing packages from delivery trucks, looting local stores and breaking into apartments. In 1919, when he was 17, he was caught during a break and enter, convicted of unlawful entry and sentenced to 13 months in the Blackwell Island Penitentiary. He was soon transferred to Westhampton Prison Farms from which he promptly escaped. He was recaptured less than 15 hours later, and two months were added to his sentence.

After spending 15 months in jail, Arthur was a hardened criminal. But it was the last time he ever spent any time behind bars, even though he would be arrested at least a dozen more times during his criminal career on a variety of charges.

Dutch Schultz, the "Beer Baron of the Bronx" was gunned down by rival gangsters at age 34. His mysterious deathbed ramblings have been immortalized in various books and movies.

~⊃Ҁ~

Upon his release, Arthur Flegenheimer adopted the name Dutch Schultz. It was the name of a once-feared brawler for a gang of young misfits called the Frog Hollow Gang. He admired and feared the gang of hoodlums that had terrorized the Bronx when he was a young man. With his newly acquired name, the tobacco-chewing pool shark with a reputation for being a penny-pincher carried on with his career as a New York gangster.

"If I'd kept the name Flegenheimer, nobody would have heard of me," he was often fond of saying.

In all likelihood, however, it wasn't Dutch Schultz's name change that put him in the gangster history books; it was Prohibition. If it weren't for America going dry in January 1920, it's likely that no one would remember Dutch Schultz. That winter, the smalltime street hood took a job driving beer trucks for his friend Charles "Lucky" Luciano.

Luciano would become one of the most powerful Mafia dons in the United States. He was born in Sicily in 1897 and immigrated to America with his family in 1906. Luciano left school at 14 and began selling heroin on the streets of New York. He rose quickly through the underworld, and by 1920, Luciano was a major power in the bootlegging rackets in New York City. Dutch watched and learned as Lucky raked in thousands of dollars supplying illegal booze to a thirsty clientele.

Lucky was looking for loyal troops, and it wasn't long before he recruited his 18-year-old pal, Dutch Schultz. Dutch had earned a reputation as a cold-blooded killer whose intimidating manner scared even the toughest gangsters. Lucky hired Schultz to muscle the booze and numbers trade out of the hands of the black gangs in Harlem who had a stranglehold on those rackets.

It wasn't long before Schultz was running his own bootlegging operation. And Dutch ruled by intimidation. He would drive into Harlem and set up a meeting with one of the black leaders. Each meeting started the same way. Schultz would walk into the room, and as he sat down, he would slowly pull out the massive .45 caliber handgun he kept tucked in his shoulder holster under his suit jacket. He'd put a bullet in the chamber, pull the hammer back and then lay it on the table in front of him.

"Nice to meet you folks, but I have some good news and some bad news," he'd say, staring the startled hood straight in the eyes. "The bad news from your point of view is that I'm taking over your operation. The good news is that if you behave yourself, I won't kill you, and you'll work for me. "

The black gangs that were running the booze operations and speakeasies in Harlem were not used to such blatant displays of violence and intimidation. They were collectors, not enforcers. They quickly agreed to this crazy white man's threats and began working for Dutch Schultz.

Dutch's quick temper, wild behavior and financial smarts earned him respect from the Syndicate. One night in 1922, during a business meeting in the Bronx, "Lucky" Luciano and Al Capone were talking mob business. At the time, Capone was orchestrating what would become the Mafia's stranglehold on crime in the Windy City. As with Schultz, Capone's relationship with Luciano went back to their childhood in Brooklyn. The two men were discussing Prohibition and the booze trade.

"We've got to get more liquor flowing from Canada," said Lucky. "The Prohibition agents are watching me too close here in New York. I hear there's good Canadian booze that's ripe for the picking.

Capone leaned forward, listening intently.

"I've got just the guy for you," Lucky said. "His name is Dutch Schultz, and he's tough as nails, smart and takes orders real good. He does have a couple of quirks about him, though."

"I'm listening," said Capone.

"He's a bit of a loon. He can go from zero to psycho in seconds, and he's one of the cheapest guys I ever knew, practically a miser," said Luciano. "Makes all this money and buys the cheapest suits around."

Capone sat back and chuckled. "I can use a guy like that."

Capone was on the lookout for tough new recruits to add to his growing army of mobsters.

"Send him out to Chicago," Capone said. "I could use some brains and street smarts in my outfit. I just need him for a couple of months. I'm going to send him north to Saskatchewan to set up a liquor deal with a couple of Canadian boys who make good whiskey."

The two men toasted the deal, and a month later, in June 1922, Dutch Schultz joined the Capone mob. Capone's Chicago gangland was a different world for Dutch. In New York you didn't kill for pleasure or anger; you only killed for business. But in Chicago, life was cheap—1000 gangland killings occurred in the Windy City between 1922 and 1932.

The Capone tough guys held the street-wise New Yorker in awe. After knowing Schultz for only a couple of weeks, one hood described him with respect.

"On the surface he was a gentleman and a scholar, but he had eyes like a reptile, and when he looked at you, he almost paralyzed you. I think he was absolutely fearless."

Schultz had been in Chicago for only a few months when Capone told him he was sending him north.

"There's a couple of Canadian brothers by the name of Bronfman who run a distillery up in Saskatchewan. I called them and told them you're coming up. You leave tomorrow."

So, at the beginning of August 1922, Schultz traveled north by train on the Soo Line to Saskatchewan to spearhead a liquor deal with Sam and Harry Bronfman.

The Bronfmans were legitimate distillers in Canada, and they, like many other Canadians, were a prime source of illicit spirits for the U.S. during Prohibition. Even though Saskatchewan brought in its own Prohibition laws in 1917, it only banned public or hotel drinking but did not prohibit the manufacture and export of liquor. The Bronfmans exploited that legal loophole and sold thousands of gallons legally to the American mobs who would then smuggle it across the border. Often they made bigger fortunes than many gangsters.

Bienfait, Saskatchewan, was only a two-and-a-half-street town in the '20s, but it was a smuggler's paradise. Only 15 miles from North Dakota, the area boasted dozens of remote roads that crossed the border. It was a favorite meeting place between Canadian bootleggers and American gangsters looking to strike a deal for Canadian whiskey. The town was easily accessible from the United States via the CPR and Soo rail lines, and it housed a major liquor storage facility and export house for the Bronfman brothers. In fact, some say the town got its name from the railroad. It's said when a French railroad worker pounded in the last spike of the day in 1889, he was heard to say "bien fait," which is French for "well done."

For a moment, standing at the Bienfait train station, Dutch Schultz had second thoughts about Capone's request to strike a major liquor deal. He wondered how this tiny prairie town could possibly be the hub of a liquor operation big enough to supply Capone's needs. Looking around at the sparse town, all he saw were two grain elevators, a general store, a Chinese laundry and a blacksmith shop. A few Model T Fords were in evidence, but mostly horses and buggies were the favorite mode of transportation. The focal point was a two-story, 10-bedroom hotel.

Schultz had been told that the Bronfman brothers were making the best whiskey around, and his job was to strike a deal to get booze flowing out of Canada and into Chicago for the Capone organization.

He walked across the street, carrying his one battered suitcase, and checked in to the White Hotel. The hotel was a favorite stopping place for locals and travelers. It was a place where men could drink, smoke, play pool and do business.

After checking in for the night, Schultz wandered down to the lounge for a drink and a bite to eat. When he walked into the restaurant, strung out from the long train ride, he could feel all eyes on him. Visitors were always a curiosity in the sleepy town, and this mysterious stranger with the thick Bronx drawl was no exception.

High-Tech Gangbusters. U.S. Federal Prohibition agents used Model Ts and biplanes to track rumrunners smuggling booze from Canada into the U.S. during Prohibition. The Model T Ford (or "tin lizzie," as it was sometimes known) was the result of the dream of automaker Henry Ford to build a rugged, simple car at a price low enough for everyone to afford. It became the most famous automobile ever built. The first Model T rolled off the assembly line in 1908 and sold for as low as $260. By the time production ceased in 1927, more than 15 million Model Ts had been built. In the early '20s, the U.S. government bought five biplanes that were used specifically in the war on whiskey smugglers. The planes were used to spot stills in the backcountry and to track the movements of rumrunners trying to smuggle hooch across state lines.

In the pool room at the back of the restaurant, a high stakes billiard or card game was always underway. Schultz noticed a big man sitting at a table by himself watching him intently. Schultz stared right back. The man motioned Dutch to join him with a finger that looked like a sausage. The man was known as Fat Earl. He owned the restaurant in the White Hotel and always offered his new customers a double or nothing gamble for the price of a meal. Schultz walked over, sat down and the two men shook hands as they introduced themselves to each other. Fat Earl was impressed with the man's firm grip.

"It's tradition in these parts to play the coin toss," Fat Earl said with a smile, pulling out a 50-cent piece from his vest pocket. "See that crack in the floor over there? All you have to do is toss the coin and make it stick in the crack. Like this."

Fat Earl flipped the coin through the air, and Schultz watched in amazement as the coin landed on its side and stuck in the crack.

"If you do the same, I'll buy ya dinner,"

Schultz laughed, "I'll give it a go."

He flipped the coin and then laughed as it missed the target and rolled down the floor.

"Never mind," said Earl. "I'll buy ya dinner anyway. Welcome to Canada. I can tell by your American accent that you're not from these parts. What brings ya to Bienfait?

Schultz chose his words carefully.

"I'm just on a little holiday to visit some Canadian friends. Thought I'd stop off here and rest up before I carry on to Moose Jaw. I hear it's a good place to gamble and have some fun. Things are pretty dull right now in Chicago with Prohibition and all."

"Well you picked the right town to rest up in before your wild time in The Jaw, " Fat Earl chuckled. "Nothing exciting ever happens here." He looked at Schultz closely.

"For a minute, I thought you might be one of those big-time gangster types, but I can see by the way you're dressed that's not the case. I always picture them in flashy expensive suits. No offense," Fat Earl added quickly.

"No offense taken," Schultz said. "Personally, I think only queers wear silk shirts. A guy's a sucker who spends 15 bucks on a shirt when you can get a good one for two."

After his colorful introduction to Fat Earl, Dutch Schultz spent the next few days wandering around town, eating at the Chinese restaurant and spending money in the local stores. He seemed to be enjoying the quaint hospitality of the prairie folks, who had no idea that the well-mannered stranger was a cold-blooded killer. He even took in a baseball game, where he bought some kids ice cream.

However, the hotel staff soon saw a dark side to this seemingly charming stranger. The chambermaid recalled walking into his room to change his bedding and towels and found Schultz napping in an easy chair by the window, his guns hanging on the bedpost. She backed out of the room nervously and quietly shut the door.

On his third day in Bienfait, Schultz phoned the Bronfman brothers who lived in Regina, arranging a meeting on the weekend to set up the liquor deal.

Harry Bronfman and his brother Sam were extremely successful businessmen and well known throughout western Canada. In 1920, the Bronfmans obtained a license for a bonded liquor warehouse in Yorkton, about 60 miles north of Bienfait. It's said that the millions of dollars they made selling booze to American gangsters spearheaded their mighty Seagram's empire in the years to come.

The brothers moved to Regina from Yorkton in 1921, but they still liked to conduct most of their booze business out of the Balmoral Hotel in Yorkton. It was in this Saskatchewan hotel that the Bronfman dynasty was born.

The Bronfman brothers were shrewd businessmen but with very different personalities. Sam had a hair-trigger temper and a blistering vocabulary of curse words. Harry, on the other hand, was shy and easygoing.

The Bronfman family was part of the exodus of more than three million Russian Jews who fled the persecution of Czarist Russia and came to Canada between 1885 and 1914. The family settled on a homestead in the Wapella, Saskatchewan area in the 1890s. The brothers struck out on their own in 1905 and moved to Yorkton, where they entered into several business ventures that proved lucrative, including real estate and pharmacies. They made huge profits in the Yorkton area from 1905 to 1915.

But the Bronfman empire really got its start when the brothers began taking advantage of loopholes in Canada's Prohibition laws. Under federal law, it was perfectly legal to ship booze from province to province, but it was illegal to ship from one point in the province to another. They formed the Yorkton Distributing Company, and using Canada's rail lines, the Bronfmans carved out a profitable liquor-shipping and mail-order business. Then, when Prohibition, "The Noble Experiment," was introduced in the United States, the two brothers kicked their whiskey-manufacturing operation into high gear.

They soon had liquor storehouses in dozens of southern Saskatchewan towns. These warehouses became known as "Boozoriums," and the locals say they were more secure than the town banks. The Bronfman's had iron bars installed on the windows and heavy locks on the doors to seal them as if they were vaults.

The brothers designed a unique blending process in their distilling operation. They bought ten 1000-gallon redwood vats for mixing the booze. They'd bring in thousands of gallons of ethyl alcohol in five-gallon metal cans, pour it into the vats and then mix in water and flavoring to taste. Sometimes caramel was used to add color to the liquor. Blackstrap molasses was added to give the booze a "rum" flavor. Then they bought a bottling machine and a labeling machine that would stick a scotch, bourbon or whiskey label on the bottle depending on the flavor. The cost for the Bronfman's to produce a case was $5.25. Rumrunners bought the booze for $50 per case.

Word spread quickly among the American bootleggers that the Bronfmans were able to supply massive quantities of high-quality booze from points in Saskatchewan, Manitoba, Ontario and Quebec. Their whiskey was soon in high demand. The amount of Bronfman liquor that flowed across the border at that time was staggering. More than 30,000 cases were exported by rail out of Yorkton every month!

The Bronfmans also knew how to stay one step ahead of the law when it came to getting the liquor to American whiskey smugglers. Instead of transporting the booze themselves, they developed a "here-it-is-come-and-get-it" style of business. They invited the smugglers to one of their many Boozoriums that were scattered throughout southern Saskatchewan, and once the money changed hands, the thugs loaded up their cars and took the risk of getting the illegal cargo across the border undetected.

The car of choice for the smugglers was the top-of-the-line Studebaker "Big Six." In 1920, this seven-passenger all-metal touring vehicle was priced at $2133. It weighed over 3000 pounds, and the heavy-duty springs made it perfect for hauling heavy loads. Its 353-cubic-inch six-cylinder engine provided over 60 horsepower and could plow through muddy Saskatchewan back roads with relative ease. The smugglers would tear out the backseats and then could load in about 40 cases of booze. Only a handful of Mounties was assigned to watch the 440-mile Saskatchewan–U.S. border, and it wasn't long before convoys of cars loaded with Bronfman booze were being driven undetected across the line and on to their American destinations.

The Bronfman brothers never intended to meet face to face with Dutch. They knew the quick-tempered goon was a violent sociopath and well connected with the American mobsters, and it would be highly risky for the RCMP to discover that they were conducting business dealings with the thug. Instead, the brothers arranged for Schultz to meet their brother-in-law and partner Paul Matoff at the White Hotel.

Matoff was well known in the area as a hard-drinking gambler and ruthless businessman who would stop at nothing to turn a profit. He was married to the Bronfmans' oldest sister and rented a home in Estevan at 1309–3rd Street. He was in charge of the Bronfman stores and Boozoriums at Gainsborough, Carnduff and Bienfait. Whenever American whiskey runners showed up in southern Saskatchewan, it was Matoff who arranged the deal.

On August 7, Paul Matoff arrived for his meeting with Schultz around 9:00 PM at the hotel. The two men met privately in Dutch's room, and in hushed tones, discussed the deal. Schultz would arrange for a couple of big cars to meet them at the Boozorium south of town at midnight. Matoff would open it up, and they'd load up the cars with Bronfman whiskey. Schultz would then leave with his boys to sneak across the border. If everything went smoothly, Dutch told Matoff, he would have his boys come back every few months and do the same deal again.

The whiskey business in the 1920s was usually done with cash before delivery. Dutch had brought a suitcase full of bundles of money, and he handed it over to Matoff. They shook hands, and Dutch presented Matoff with a $10,000 diamond stickpin as a show of good faith. Matoff wore the pin every day after as a good-luck charm. The two men then quietly left town and drove the half hour south to the Boozorium.

Dutch's boys were waiting in the dark on the side road leading into the warehouse. They quickly loaded up the cars, and Dutch and his men drove off into the Saskatchewan night headed for the border.

Two months after his meeting with Dutch Schultz, Paul Matoff's shady dealings with American gangsters came to an abrupt and bloody end.

Paul met with another American gangster late one night in October 1922 near a deserted granary six miles east of Bienfait. It was about 10:30 PM, and the light was growing dim. It was a typical liquor deal that Matoff had done many times before. The American gave Matoff $1680 cash in a briefcase in exchange for 12 barrels of liquor that had been transferred from a warehouse to a truck parked nearby on the gravel road.

Everything was going smoothly on that night. The men talked about the weather and new cars and shared a drink from a flask. At this point, the details are sketchy, but pleasantries quickly turned to anger, and the deal went sour. Someone pulled a sawed-off shotgun out and killed Matoff with a single blast to the chest. He was dead before he hit the ground and was found the next morning, sprawled out flat on his back with his arms outstretched on the blood-soaked prairie sod. His good-luck charm, the diamond stickpin Schultz had given him, was gone.

To this day, the brutal killing has never been solved, and the briefcase of money and diamond stickpin were never recovered. A Canadian, Jimmy LaCoste, and an American, Lee Dillage, were charged but later found not guilty. Some believe that the man behind the staged hold-up was Dutch Schultz, but it was never proven.

Once Dutch had set up the Bronfman deal in Bienfait for Al Capone, and the booze pipeline was flowing freely from Saskatchewan into Chicago, the mobster headed to New York State where he set up his own operation. It's believed he returned to Saskatchewan at least two more times in the '20s to spearhead more booze-smuggling deals. More than one person in southern Saskatchewan recalls seeing the American mobster checking into hotels in Bienfait and Moose Jaw.

In New York, Dutch carried on his bootlegging and racketeering business with the blessing of his mentor Lucky Luciano. He set up his illegal business in Patchogue, Long Island. The area quickly became a dangerous place. Honest citizens soon found it to their advantage to ignore the after-dark dealings on the local beaches. Long Island began to look like a war zone. Gun battles between rival bootleggers and federal agents were front-page news. It was becoming commonplace to find gangsters' bodies, riddled with bullets, dumped on beaches and roads.

Dutch Schultz quickly expanded his operation with a pal named Joe Noe. The two set up their first small speakeasy at 543 Brook Avenue, New York. They bought four old moving vans, converted them into beer trucks and put together a ruthless band of outlaws. Dutch lived up to his reputation as a miser. He kept close tabs on his accountants and frequently checked the books himself. His drivers and triggermen often grumbled that they were overworked and underpaid, but they also knew that asking for a raise could send the gang leader into a psychotic fit of rage.

One of his men described him, "You can insult Dutch's girl, spit in his face and push him around, and he'll laugh. But don't steal a dollar from his accounts. If you do, you're dead."

The hood wasn't exaggerating.

One evening in 1928, while counting up the day's gambling receipts in the hotel room he used as an office, he noticed a discrepancy in his accounting book. He immediately accused Jules Martin, the man who was in charge of his numbers racket, of stealing from him.

"I'm missing $20,000," he yelled, slapping Martin's face several times. "You're the rat who took it, aren't you?"

A shaken Martin quickly confessed and promised to return the money.

"It's too late, you chiseler," was all Dutch said.

He pulled out his .45, stuffed the barrel into Jules' mouth, looked into the terrified man's eyes and pulled the trigger.

Schultz ordered his men to take the body and throw it into a ditch out of town. He also told them to stab the body several times as a warning to other would-be thieves.

Despite Dutch's outlaw band of gangsters, his illegal operations were rapidly and often violently expanding throughout New York State. By the end of the 1920s, Dutch owned speakeasies all over the Bronx and Manhattan. By selling beer to rival gangs, Dutch and his partner Joe Noe took control of the city's best cabarets and blind pigs. The move was business genius, and their profits increased dramatically. If the gangsters' offer to buy bootleg booze was turned down, Dutch and Noe simply out-muscled the competition. They ruled by intimidation.

One rival gang that made the fatal mistake of trying to move in on Dutch and Noe's operation was run by two brothers, Joe and John Rock. They were stubborn Irishmen who refused to let Schultz stand in their way. One night, Schultz's boys kidnapped Joe and took him to an abandoned warehouse on the Upper East Side. They strung him up on meat hooks and wrapped a gauze bandage contaminated with gonorrhea over his eyes. As the mobster struggled, they rubbed the bandage deep into his eye sockets until he screamed in pain. After two hours, the Schultz gang dropped Joe off on a quiet street in Manhattan. Within five days, Joe Rock went blind—a living testimonial to anyone who tried to mess with Schultz and Noe.

The brutality of the incident created fear and loathing among the other gangs, and they left Schultz free to expand his operation. Outlaws and street thugs lined up to join Schultz's team, and his empire quickly grew as he took on more orders for bootleg booze.

But Schultz's New York dynasty took him into direct contact with yet another powerful gang run by Jack "Legs" Diamond. Like Schultz, Diamond was unpredictable and feared by the New York underworld. But when Schultz began moving in on Diamond's turf, a violent mob war began for control of the New York bootleg trade.

Early one October morning in 1928, Diamond's men sat parked in a blue Cadillac outside the Chateau Madrid nightclub on West 54th street. As Noe walked out of the club, Diamond's hit man Louis Weinberg fired a single blast from his sawed-off shotgun at Noe from the backseat window. Even though Noe was wearing a bulletproof vest, the hail of buckshot tore into his neck and legs. Noe pulled out his .38 as he crumpled to the sidewalk and emptied the gun into his attacker. As he lay bleeding on the sidewalk, the car roared away. When police found the abandoned Cadillac on the outskirts of town later that day, they discovered the body of Louis Weinberg in the backseat. Joe Noe got his revenge before he passed on.

Schultz was crushed by his old friend's death, and he hungered for revenge. Another round of bloodshed began on November 4, 1928. Schultz arranged a hit on Legs Diamond's money man and good friend, Arnold Rothstein. They gunned him down in the Park Central Hotel, and he died two days later.

Next he set his sights on Legs Diamond himself. Diamond had just been acquitted on a kidnapping charge in Syracuse, New York. He had been celebrating at a drunken party and ended up at the house of his girlfriend, Kiki Roberts. They were naked in bed when the door was kicked open, and two of Schultz's boys burst in with guns blazing. Diamond sat straight up in shock at the sight, but before he could utter a cry for help or reach for his pistol, the bullets from the tommy guns cut him in two.

The violence kicked off an entire month of gangland violence. Rival gangs began tearing apart Dutch's organization. In one incident of extreme violence, members of the Coll Gang burst into a room where Schultz's mobsters were playing cards, and they shot everyone in sight. They tried to machine-gun one of Schultz's main men, Joe Rao, but they shot wide and ended up killing a five-year-old boy who got caught in the crossfire.

The battle for territory was on. It was the Dutch Schultz mob versus the Coll Gang. Peter "Mad Dog" Coll, his brother Vincent and their men unleashed a barrage of attacks on the Schultz outfit.

The Coll Gang wrecked Schultz's booze warehouses and smashed his slot machines. Dutch retaliated by lighting Coll's speakeasies and beer trucks on fire. Blood flowed in the streets.

Local headlines read: Seven Dead in Schultz-Coll War. Then it was 12, 20, and by 1932, the death toll reached as high as 50!

"If we don't kill these goons, Peter and Vincent, our business is finished," Schulz muttered to his top henchman.

The first hit planned was on Peter. On May 30, two of Schultz's triggermen staked out his apartment. As Peter came out of his rooming house, the two gunmen fell in behind him as he walked down the street. After following him for about a block, the two men looked up and down the street. Seeing that all was clear, they called out.

"Hey Pete, look out behind ya."

Peter turned around and saw the two henchmen walking quickly toward him.

"Wadda ya want," he snarled and then spit on the sidewalk, his hand going to his breast pocket.

Within seconds, gunfire exploded on the quiet street. Peter Coll was dead before he hit the ground, as bullets from the tommy guns ripped through his body. The smell of gunpowder filled the air, and the hired killers calmly walked to a waiting car and drove away.

Vincent took Peter's murder hard. In retaliation he had four of Schultz's men gunned down in the streets in the next few weeks. The gang war reached its peak.

The deadly battle with gangsters killing gangsters wasn't over. Next on the list was Vincent. On February 9, 1932, the Schultz gang tracked him down to a drugstore at 86 College Avenue. Vincent was talking on the phone in the back of the pharmacy. One man stayed outside in a blue Cadillac, another waited at the door, while another walked in and pulled a sawed-off shotgun out of his trench coat. He made a downward motion with his hand to the druggist.

"Hit the floor, buddy."

Vincent didn't even know what hit him. The Schultz gun-man walked up to Coll, who was in the middle of a heated discussion on the phone, his back to the room. The assassin pointed the barrel of a sawed-off shotgun about a foot from the back of Vincent's head and pulled the trigger. Vincent's head exploded and stained the wall a bright crimson. He crumpled to the floor, still holding the phone in his left hand. Blood and brains slid down the wall and into the growing dark puddle on the floor under his body. The killer spun around and calmly walked out the door and into the waiting Caddy. When police arrived a few minutes later, they were only able identify the murdered gangster whose head and face was blown apart by the single 410 shotgun shell by a dry-cleaning stub in his pocket.

The bloodshed continued until Dutch had either killed or scared off all his competition. He now had a private army of more than 100 expert gunmen. These men were not like the flashy gangsters of the early '20s. These were urban guerillas, phantom menaces who lived in the shadows and answered only to Dutch Schultz.

It was during this time that an intriguing legend was born about Dutch Schultz and millions of dollars in buried treasure.

Many of Schultz's gangster friends who'd been sentenced to hard time found themselves broke when they got out of prison. Schultz came up with a plan to ensure that never happened to him. He had an ironworker make him a steel chest in which he could stash the millions he had hoarded over the years. Some say the chest contained over $5 million in gold, diamonds and cash.

Schultz had the steel box loaded into his car, and he and his friend Lu Lu Rosenkrantz drove to upstate New York, to the Catskills near the town of Phoenicia.

According to one old-timer, the Dutchman and Rosenkrantz stopped for lunch at the Phoenicia Hotel. The two gangsters created quite a stir in the sleepy resort town. After lunch, they drove north out of town on Route 214, following the Stony Clove Creek for about eight miles. Turning off the road, they drove into a grove of pine trees beneath a skull-rock formation called the Devil's Face. Grunting and sweating, the two men dragged the treasure chest into the grove, dug a hole and buried the fortune. They must have felt almost like modern-day pirates.

Years later, Rosenkrantz supposedly made a map of where the loot was buried, and a gangster who saw the directions said they'd even marked an "X" on the tree above where the loot was hidden. After Rosenkrantz's death, the map disappeared, and the legend of the buried treasure's location continued to grow. To this day it has never been found.

Back in New York City, Schultz's reign was being challenged from many fronts. If it wasn't rival gangsters trying to gun him down and take over his territory, the law was always close behind. So far, he'd avoided arrest by paying off police and politicians in the usual gangster tradition.

But it was tax evasion charges that eventually brought him down. After he beat one federal tax evasion rap in 1933, he faced a similar charge in 1935. These cases were assembled by

Thomas Dewey (1902–71) was an aggressive U.S. prosecuting attorney whose successful racket-busting career won him three terms as governor of New York (1943–55).

Thomas Dewey, the special prosecutor who was heading the task force against organized crime.

Dewey was born in 1902, and he graduated from the University of Michigan in 1923. After receiving his law degree at Columbia University, he worked for well-known New York City law firms and eventually entered the political arena. In the 1930s, he was appointed special prosecutor to investigate organized crime in New York City. He became a household name in the U.S. for successfully sending several mob bosses to prison and some to the electric chair. In later years, he became governor of New York and worked for the Republican Party until his death in Florida in 1971.

Dewey's reputation as a shrewd and aggressive lawyer who went on a public crusade to cripple organized crime made Schultz and his lawyers wary. They knew that the tenacious special prosecutor would put together a tough case against the mobster. Witnesses came forward with details of Schultz's earnings. Some of his financial records, so meticulously documented in his account books, were to be used as evidence. Federal tax evasion charges would be difficult to beat. But what made Schultz's defense team even more nervous was when the government moved the trial out of New York City. The United States justice system didn't want to take any chances that Schultz would use his corrupt ring of political power in New York to buy his freedom. To Schultz's dismay, he would have to defend himself in the tiny town of Malone, New York. Schultz's gangland friends believed the Dutchman's mob days would soon be over, and that he would be locked up for a long time.

Once again, the Dutchman surprised everyone. He spent his time in Malone while awaiting trial mingling with the local folks, who found the so-called ruthless mobster and cold-blooded killer to be charming and generous. He stayed at the Hotel Flanigan and was constantly seen around town, spending a lot of money in the local shops and restaurants. He bought toys for sick kids at the hospital and often picked up everyone's tab when he was paying his restaurant bill. He also took steps to convert to Catholicism in the town's tiny Catholic Church and joined the congregation for Mass on Sundays.

His schmoozing worked. On August 2, 1935, the jury, after deliberating for 28 hours and 23 minutes, brought in a verdict of not guilty.

Dutch Schultz Wanted Poster, January 1934. The New York mobster went into hiding after the U.S. Federal Government charged him with income tax evasion.

~•❀•~

But Prosecutor Thomas Dewey wasn't ready to give up. Just weeks after Schultz returned to New York from his trial in Malone, Dewey, who was now a district attorney, charged the mobster again, this time for state tax evasion.

Dutch Schultz exploded with rage. "This is the last straw!" he screamed. "I want that son of a bitch dead."

He called a meeting between the New York gang leaders and demanded that the Syndicate order Dewey's assassination. He asked Lucky Luciano to order his elite squad of mob killers, called Murder, Incorporated, to kill Dewey. The gang leaders were shocked. Lucky Luciano immediately refused, explaining that Dewey was far too high profile for a mob hit. It was obvious to everyone but Schultz that killing a district attorney would bring the full force of the law down on the mob and cripple their business.

When the Syndicate voted down Schultz's request to assassinate Dewey, the enraged gangster turned to Luciano and spat on the surprised mob boss. He looked around the room in disgust at his cohorts.

"If that's the way it's going to be, I'll kill the bastard myself." He marched out the door.

Realizing that Schultz was out of control, the Syndicate decided the crazy Dutchman would have to be killed before he could murder Dewey. Schultz had just signed his own death warrant.

Luciano ordered Murdered, Incorporated's top gunmen to carry out the hit on Dutch Schultz. He specifically asked for Charles "the Bug" Workman, Emanuel "Mendy" Weiss and the driver, a man affectionately known as "Piggy," to get rid of Schultz.

Piggy sat behind the wheel. He was so fat that he had the seat in the Ford sedan custom made to accommodate his heavy frame. Mendy sat beside him with Workman in the back—a cool killer with dark, curly hair and cold, metal blue eyes.

The triggermen decided that the hit would take place at a restaurant called the Palace Chop House in Newark, New Jersey, where Dutch had set up headquarters. On October 23, Schultz was dining in the back of the Chop House with three of his men—Lu Lu Rosenkrantz, Otto "Abbaddabba" Berman and Abe "Misfit" Landau. Once or twice a week, they met at the restaurant on Park Street to go over the day's business. About halfway through the meal, Dutch went to the washroom.

Outside, Workman and Weiss got out of the idling car as Piggy stayed behind the wheel. Both men drew their revolvers as they walked into the restaurant and calmly began walking toward the back. Halfway down the bar, they raised their pistols and began blasting at the three men sitting at the table in the corner.

Lu Lu, who was sitting with his back to the doorway, was hit seven times. Berman was blown off his chair as six slugs tore into his body. Landau was hit three times. He went down but came up shooting after pulling a .45 automatic out of his shoulder holster. But his bullets went wild, and he dropped unconscious to the restaurant floor.

When he didn't see Schultz, Workman went into the men's room and found Dutch hiding in a washroom stall. Workman fired twice. One bullet hit Schultz, wounding him.

Workman ran out the front door where Weiss was waiting for him. They jumped in the car, and "Piggy" drove away.

Schultz staggered out of the men's room and collapsed at one of the tables.

"Somebody call a doctor, I'm hit bad."

Rosenkrantz, who was badly wounded, somehow managed to sit up and throw a dime to the Chop House owner, telling him to call a doctor. He then collapsed unconscious on the floor.

What's amazing about the hit was not the precision and timing with which it was carried out, but that in the barrage of bullets none of the gangsters died at the scene.

The four men were rushed by ambulance to the City Hospital on Fairmount Street in Newark. Police officers and reporters surrounded them, all shouting questions at the wounded gangsters. One local news photographer even stuck his foot under the wheel of Schultz's gurney as he was being carted into the emergency ward and demanded a quick photo.

Schultz snarled, " What's more important, your picture or my life? Get outta here!"

Dutch was taken to the emergency room where a nurse started to cut off his bloody clothes so that the doctors could dress the wounds. Even though he was in terrible pain, he reached into his pocket and pulled out a wad of bills. With a shaking hand, he pressed the cash into the surprised young lady's hand.

"There's over $700 there," he whispered. "Make sure they treat me good."

Schultz was in bad shape. A rusty steel-jacketed .45 bullet had torn a hole through his body. It had ripped through his left side, down into his stomach then through his intestines, gall-bladder and liver. He had massive internal bleeding and an infection. The doctors knew Schultz's time on earth was running out. They gave him a shot of morphine and patched him up as best they could.

As doctors worked on Schultz, Landau and Berman were pronounced dead. They never regained consciousness after the shooting and bled to death from their gunshot wounds.

Rosenkrantz, however, was still alive. Detectives began interrogating the wounded gangster as doctors tried to patch him up, but he wasn't in any mood for questions. He'd lost a lot of blood, and his lungs and internal organs had been ripped to shreds by the seven slugs. He kept asking for an ice cream soda. Eventually, the police gave up their questioning. Rosenkrantz would last the longest of the four men. He died at 3:20 AM on October 25, 30 hours after he was gunned down.

Schultz, meanwhile, drifted in and out of consciousness throughout the night, and early in the morning he started to mumble in strange, babbling phrases.

"Whose number is what you hear it on my shoes off. Oh, instead hold it takes all right, police, look out for the book. You pick up? I would be spoken about. Winnifred. Say…police are only thing that with it on, oh, look out! French-Canadian bean soup. "

The police assigned a court stenographer and a policeman to his bedside to see if he might reveal who shot him and why.

The stenographer recorded every last bizarre word and phrase the gangster uttered.

"Old pal of mine. Come on, come over here! Come on, so get your onions up and we will throw up the truce flag…Police are here, cut that out! If you have in the department. All right, look out! My shoes. There are 10 million fighting somewhere of you, please take me out. Pardon me, I won't be such a nickel to two guys like you or me, but to a week fight. No business. No business. No! Come on, I am I doing here with my collection of papers. It is no use to go there. I don't. I forgot that I will have done it, please, warden. Nothing. Just pull out and give me water, the boy came at me."

Schultz regained consciousness, and he asked for a priest. Schultz wanted to die a Catholic. Father Cornelius McInerney baptized him and gave Schultz the last rites of the Roman Catholic Church.

His wife, Frances Flegenheimer, and his mother, Emma, visited and were visibly rattled by Schultz's bizarre ramblings. Frances was a slender and pretty 21-year-old, auburn-haired woman who wore thick glasses. The two met when she was just 18 and working as a hatcheck girl in a speakeasy in New York's Maison Royal. She was the mother of his two children.

When questioned by police, Schultz's gray-haired mother claimed she had no idea of her son's criminal dealings.

"I saw him just a month ago," she said. "He was happy and healthy, always a good boy."

Although some of Schultz's rantings may have referred to his shooting and criminal activities, most seemed to be about old rhymes and songs and childhood memories.

"Oh, oh dog biscuit, and when he is happy he doesn't get snappy," he muttered.

Some people believe that parts of Dutch's babble were directly related to the buried treasure he and Rosenkrantz had buried up in the Catskills.

At one point he rambled on about Satan, a possible connection to the Devil's Face rock, which it is believed he used as a landmark for his buried loot.

"Mother is the best bet, and don't let Satan draw you too fast," he said.

A few minutes later, he said, "I know what I am doing here with my collection of papers, for crying out loud. It isn't worth a nickel to two guys like you or me, but to a collector it is worth a fortune; it is priceless. I am going to turn it over to…"

As his condition worsened and his fever increased, he began to drift in and out of consciousness, often babbling strange and disconnected phrases such as, "The glove will fit what I say," and "The sidewalk was in trouble, and the bears were in trouble." The authorities kept a stenographer at Schultz's bedside to record every last rambling thought he uttered. Federal agents and police from New York and New Jersey tried in vain to analyze his last words after his death.

Dutch Schultz lasted until 8:30 on the evening of Thursday, October 24, 1935. The Dutchman was dead at 34 years old. His death certificate lists Arthur Flegenheimer's occupation as "salesman."

On October 28, Schultz went for one last ride. Around 8:00 AM, thousands of people crowded outside the Coughlin and Brothers Funeral Home for a glimpse of the gangster in his simple chestnut coffin, but they went away disappointed. Two hours earlier, some of his gang members had paid off the funeral director and secretly taken his body to a Catholic cemetery 25 miles north of New York City.

Only three mourners were at the gravesite, his wife Frances, his mother and his sister, Mrs. Helen Ursprung. Father McInerney performed a 15-minute service, his mother placed her shawl on her son's grave and the mourners went home.

Considering the Dutchman had raked in over $800,000 in the weeks prior to his death, and his yearly income was estimated at over $20 million, it was a simple and inexpensive funeral. The total cost including cemetery plot, coffin and service was only $1200.

To this day no one is certain what became of Schultz's vast fortune. His young widow, Frances, was left to raise their two children on her own. When police investigated her finances after Dutch's murder, all they could find was a $2500 insurance policy that named her the beneficiary. She'd even paid the premiums herself and claimed she had no knowledge of other funds. They did find a bank account in Schultz's name, but it only contained $5000. Frances and her mother-in-law ended up going to court in a bitter dispute over who would get the money. In the end, it was split evenly between the two.

Shortly after Schultz's death, Frances moved her two children west to California to avoid publicity. It's believed she changed their names because they were never heard from again.

There is speculation that the miserly Schultz stashed his millions in security boxes and private vaults hidden away from the taxman and from his greedy gang members and girlfriends. Perhaps he intended to save the money for his retirement or to leave it to his family, but he was gunned down in his evil prime before he could make arrangements. One thing is certain, the thrifty Dutchman did not give his money away.

The whereabouts of Dutch's fortune is still a million-dollar mystery that has frustrated treasure hunters from Saskatchewan to New York. Every few years, a map surfaces claiming to point the way to Schultz's riches, but no treasure has ever been found. Today, the location of the gangster's millions is still a dark secret that remains buried with the Dutchman in the Gate of Heaven Cemetery in Hawthorne, New Jersey.

CHAPTER THREE

The Purple Gang

"The whole rhythm section was
the Purple Gang...Let's Rock."

–from *Jailhouse Rock* by Elvis Presley

THE '20S ROARED INTO WINDSOR, ONTARIO, like the wild notes blasting out of Louis Armstrong's battered trumpet. The bloodiest war in the history of the world was over, and the men returning from overseas were looking for excitement and a quick buck. The nation was celebrating.

It was an era when men slicked back their hair like silent movie heartthrob Rudolph Valentino, many city folk drove Model T Fords, Lucky Strikes and Chesterfields were the popular cigarettes and ladies affected kiss curls. It was an age when people washed their clothes with Lux in cold-water hand-ringer washers and at night danced the Charleston at the local roadhouse or listened to Duke Ellington on an RCA Radiola. Of course, alcohol played a big part in the festivities.

Across the river from Windsor was the Motor City—Detroit, Michigan. The Detroit River was one of the busiest waterways in the world. Massive lake freighters powered by powerful coal-fired engines steamed through loaded with timber, grain, iron ore, limestone and cement. In some places, the river was only one-half mile across. Standing on the docks in Windsor, a person could easily see the city of Detroit. But beneath the smoky skyline, violence permeated the heart of Motor City.

This was also the era of The Purple Gang, the most notorious outlaw organization to ever come out of Detroit. The gang started out as a group of juvenile delinquents, 16 or 17 children, who terrorized their Jewish neighborhood on the lower east side of Detroit. The band of misfits was founded by Joe, Abe, Raymond and Izzy Bernstein. The boys were raised in poverty by hardworking immigrant parents. They craved the good life, and stealing seemed to be the quickest way to get it. At first, they were involved in petty crime—rolling drunks and stealing from hucksters. But they quickly graduated from petty street crimes to armed robbery and hijacking. They became notorious for their ruthless and savage dealings with their enemies and even began to prey on their fellow neighbors and immigrants.

"The boys snatched ice cream, gum, candy, cookies and fruit from hucksters and stores," wrote one *Detroit Free Press* writer at the time. "They ganged up on children their own age; sometimes they strong-armed grownups."

No one is really sure how the gang first got its name, but it's believed to have been coined in these early days. One theory is that after the hoodlums pulled off a robbery in a local marketplace that left two shopkeepers battered and bruised, one merchant was said to complain to another: "These boys are not like other children of their age; they're tainted, off-color."

"Yes," another agreed. "They're rotten, purple, like the color of bad meat. They're a purple gang."

But the boyhood petty crimes were about to come to an end. A controversial American government experiment in 1920 would catapult the boys into full-blown mobsters. It was Prohibition that really got the Purple Gang organized.

On January 16, 1920, the 18th Amendment banned the sale, manufacture or transportation of liquor in the U.S.

Overnight an era of bootleg booze fueled by gangster violence and the lure of huge profits was born.

Detroit was one of the first American cities with a population of over 500,000 to enact the Prohibition law. It was the perfect opportunity for the young hoods in the Purple Gang. Detroit was only a mile from Windsor, Ontario, where liquor was readily available from the Canadian export docks. Although Ontario had a Prohibition law, it was not as heavily enforced as the U.S. law. The Liquor Control Act of Ontario banned public or hotel drinking but did not prohibit the manufacture and export of liquor. As a result, it was not illegal to export liquor to countries that did have Prohibition, so just about anyone with a boat could motor over to Ontario, buy as much liquor as he could carry and smuggle that load of prime Canadian whiskey into Michigan…if he had the guts.

The Purple Gang seized the opportunity. Not only did these young thugs have the guts to try to outsmart U.S. Customs, they also gained a fearful reputation as being ruthless and predatory. It wasn't long before the gangsters had a river of whiskey flowing across the Canadian border. They would even hijack rival whiskey smugglers they came upon on the Detroit River, steal their cargo, gun them down and then dump the bodies into the black waters.

For the border cities of Windsor, Sarnia and Detroit, Prohibition set the stage for the most violent decade ever seen. When Michigan state banned alcohol, the Purples turned to the more serious crimes of rum-running and hijacking liquor. It was during this time that the Purple Gang also earned the nickname the "Third Avenue Navy" or the "Little Jewish Navy" from their nighttime excursions back and forth across the river carrying booze from Canada and hijacking the booty of other bootleggers.

The Purple's well-oiled smuggling and hijacking operations turned the border waterways into their own smugglers' paradise for bootleg booze. The money filling up the gangsters' bank accounts boggles the mind even by today's standards. By the mid-1920s, the value of the Purple Gang's bootleg business from Canada to Detroit was estimated to be more than $250 million a year.

By 1923, the Purple Gang had more than 50 members. The gang's kingpins, Joe, Abe, Raymond and Izzy Bernstein, wielded so much power that they were even able to tell Al Capone to stay out of Michigan. Capone would have liked nothing more than to set up operation in Motor City. The blue-collar town with its large hardworking, hard-partying workforce would have been ideal for his booze and gambling rackets.

But in a high-level meeting at the Leland Hotel in downtown Detroit on August 22, 1924, Capone wisely decided it was better to have the Purples as his liquor agents than his enemies.

"Hey, I don't want no war, with you or nobody else," Capone told the Bernstein brothers, "I got my own setup. I just came over to do you guys a favor. I want to purchase some good whiskey."

So "Scarface" bought case after case of Canadian Club Whiskey from the Purples in Detroit and then shipped it to Chicago where he sold it under his "Old Log Cabin" label. For the next 17 years, the Purple Gang ruthlessly controlled the entire Detroit-Windsor area.

The Purples created a booze pipeline using Lake Erie, Lake St. Clair and the St. Clair River as the passageway for their speedboats. The vast and complex maze of islands and channels offered the perfect hiding places for the gangsters' boats. The Purples had the fastest boats afloat and could easily outrun the Canadian and American Coast Guard cutters. It's estimated that an incredible 75 percent of the liquor supplied to the United States during Prohibition was smuggled via these Canadian waterways.

The pipeline operated 24 hours a day, 7 days a week, all year long. The docks on the Canadian side were covered by simple frame sheds that dotted every possible location from Lake St. Clair to Lake Erie along the Detroit River. These sheds were used primarily to store crates of shipping goods and to protect them from the weather. The Purple Gang turned many of the sheds into secret loading areas where rumrunners could quietly load liquor onto their boats out of sight of the law. Many Canadian dock owners made thousands of American dollars renting their sheds to the Purple Gang.

The powerful speedboats then slipped across the river to Wyandotte or Ecorse on the Michigan side, there to unload the booze onto waiting trucks, which would transport the illegal cargo into Detroit where it was sold and distributed to thirsty customers nationwide.

Although a majority of citizens on both sides of the border supported Prohibition, many others refused to obey the anti-liquor laws. As a result, normally law-abiding citizens made some quick cash helping the Purple Gang keep the whiskey flowing through the booze pipeline.

One of those men was W.A. Guilfoyle, a mechanic who lived in Sarnia, Ontario, about 40 miles north of Detroit on the St. Claire River. Sarnia is a deepwater port and capable of accommodating ships from all over the world. It was along the St. Claire River that the Purple Gang smuggled thousands of gallons of prime Canadian booze.

W.A. Guilfoyle was considered one of the best mechanics in the area. The 22-year-old owned and operated Guilfoyle's Garage and Machine Shop in Sarnia on Federal Lane. It was torn down in 1948, and the post office now stands in the spot where the garage used to be. W.A. was a big man, standing nearly 6' tall and weighing 230 pounds. He had a reputation for being a hardworking family man, and he was married with two children.

W.A., as friends and family called him, was working late in his shop one August night. He was under a customer's Pierce

W.A. Guilfoyle (far left) (1885–49) with his family. He was a well-known mechanic in Sarnia, Ontario, hired by the Purple Gang to maintain the engines on their smuggling speedboats.

Arrow making a last-minute check on the brake linings he'd installed, when he heard the shop door open and footsteps on the cement floor. Thinking it must be a friend dropping by the closed shop, he pulled himself out from under the car and was startled to see two strangers standing by the bumper of the car.

"Sorry, we're closed," W.A. said to the men, as he stood up.

The two men were dressed in expensive suits. One was mopping his brow with a handkerchief and holding a fedora.

"We're from Detroit, and our boat broke down. We need a mechanic to come down to the dock and get her going."

"I'm closed for the night," W.A. repeated.

"We're willing to pay double, if you'll come down to the docks at midnight and get our boat running. We have to be back in Detroit by dawn," the man with the handkerchief said softly.

"Well that's a hard offer to turn down," W.A. said, wiping his hands with a rag. He could tell from the men's accents that they were Americans. He suspected they were rumrunners.

"Triple the money, and I'll meet you there at midnight," W.A. said.

The men agreed and walked out the door. W.A. turned out the lights, locked the door and began walking home. He chuckled to himself. Last week he'd fixed a Coast Guard cutter, and tonight he was going to fix an outlaw's boat. A job was a job, he told himself.

He went home and had supper. After his children were in bed, he told his wife that he had a late night job down by the docks and should be back by 2:00 AM.

"You be careful what you get yourself into with these gangster types," she told him, as he left the house at 11:30 for the docks.

W.A. headed down to the St. Claire waterfront. At precisely midnight, he noticed a light flashing from a boat anchored a short distance out in the harbor. The boat was typical of the type that rumrunners used to stay one step ahead of the Coast Guard. It was a 34-foot modified Sterling Viking powered by a powerful 12-cylinder aircraft engine.

W.A. rowed out to meet it. As he handed up his toolbox and climbed aboard, he noticed the boat's deck was loaded with hundreds of cases of liquor.

"What seems to be the problem, boys?" W.A. asked the five shady-looking characters on deck.

"She won't turn over, and we've gotta get back before dawn. If you get her fixed in a jiffy, there'll be an extra 50 bucks in it for ya."

W.A. went below to look at the engine and asked one of the mobsters to hold the light. He noticed that the engine was encased in a large drum that acted as a silencer, almost eliminating any engine sound. The boat had also been painted gunmetal gray so that it would be almost invisible on the water. There was even a 45-gallon drum of oil that could be poured into the exhaust to create a smoke screen so that they could disappear from the lawmen.

After a quick inspection, he saw the problem. The spark plugs were fouled. He pulled them out and had them cleaned and gapped within the hour.

"That should do it. Let's fire her up and see if she goes."

After only a couple of cranks, the 12-cylinder engine roared to life.

"There ya go. I'll leave you boys to it. Have a nice trip."

W.A. got up to leave but was quickly stopped with a snub-nosed Smith and Wesson stuck in his face.

"Hate to do this to you W.A., but we're not taking any chances. You're coming with us to make sure this boat makes it the 40 miles to Detroit."

The boat was already moving out into the river toward Walpole Island, when W.A. decided he was having none of it. He bolted down to the engine room and pulled all the wires out. Everything went silent, including the stunned gangsters.

"If you boys think I'm riding with you to Detroit, you can forget it. Promise me you'll take me back to Canada, and I'll get her running again. Otherwise, we'll sit here and drift, and it won't be long before the customs guys pick you up. I'm sure they'll be interested in your cargo on deck there."

The gangsters were on a strict time line, so they had no choice but to accede to W.A.'s gutsy request. W.A. got the boat running again, and the hoods took him back to where his row-boat was anchored. He scrambled off the boat, and the gang-sters gave the engine full throttle and disappeared into the night, leaving W.A. hanging on for dear life as the wake from the cruiser almost swamped his tiny rowboat.

Many would say that W.A. had more guts than brains to stand up to the ruthless mobsters. Many weren't so lucky.

With money comes greed, and with greed, bloodshed. The Purples didn't let anyone get in their way. They despised any kind of publicity, but when some Purple members discovered that a Canadian newspaper was doing an exposé on them, they decided to fight back.

Windsor Daily Star news photographer Horace Wilde had firsthand experience with the Purples that would haunt him until the day he died. He was assigned to take pictures at one of the docks for a bootlegging story. It was a chilly April evening. Wilde was shooting his first roll of film when he was attacked and beaten, and his camera smashed. The thugs didn't stop there. They bound, gagged and kidnapped him and would have killed him if a policeman walking by hadn't stopped the violence. The cop caught and arrested one of the hoodlums, who he was eventually convicted of kidnapping.

The Purple Gang may have been ruthless in their quest for profit, but they were cautious as well. Rather than risk getting caught by Prohibition agents, they sometimes hired enterpris-ing Canadians to do their dirty work for them. The lure of thousands of dollars in tax-free American money made work-ing for the mob highly attractive to a handful of unscrupulous Ontario businessmen despite the high risk.

One of those men was Harry Low. He was well known and well liked in the Windsor area, a legitimate businessman who successfully dabbled in real estate and the entertainment industry. But what made Low a multi-millionaire during the '20s was running liquor into the U.S. for the Purple Gang. Low was a gregarious, easygoing man who liked to laugh and tell a joke. A big, burly fellow with thick, black hair and a round, smiling face, he was the son of an Ottawa machinist. And with the Purple Gang as his main client, Low, while still in his early 40s, soon became the king of one of the biggest rum-running operations in Canada.

Harry got his start when he bought a pool hall on Sandwich Street in Windsor. He was often seen standing outside on a summer evening smoking his pipe and chatting to people out for a walk. Low knew a lot of people in Windsor—some good, some bad. And one evening a man, who Low knew often operated outside the law, approached him.

"Hey Harry, I've got a fat cat from Detroit says he wants to meet you with a business deal that sounds kinda sweet," the man said. "Looks like there could be a lot of money in it."

"Always interested in a good business deal," Low said. "Set it up. Never hurts to hear what's up."

Harry had a hunch that the deal involved booze. It was well known around Windsor that Harry dabbled in the liquor business and liked to make a quick buck. One of his acquaintances was James Cooper, who was a head salesmen for the Hiram Walker Distillery in nearby Walkerville. Low could always count on Cooper to make sure he always had a big stockpile of Hiram Walker's finest Canadian Club whiskey stored in the basement of his pool hall to serve up to his patrons. Often those patrons included American gangsters staying in town to cut deals with Canadian bootleggers. So he wasn't surprised when the mob approached him to get involved in the smuggling operation. The meeting was set for 10:00 PM on July 6, 1924. He was to meet the gangsters nine miles out of town on the outskirts of Tecumseh, Ontario.

Harry drove to the meeting by himself in his Model T Ford. When he got to the place, he saw a black sedan pulled over on a side road with its lights out and engine running. He was nervous as he got out of his car and walked over to the driver's side. The window rolled down two inches.

"Get in, Mr. Low," said a gruff voice with an American accent.

Low walked around the front of the car and got in the front passenger's side. Another man was sitting in the backseat smoking a cigarette.

"Nice to meet you Mr. Low," the driver said. "My name is Eddie Fletcher. That's Nicki Steinburg in the back. We want to make you an offer that I think you'll find hard to refuse."

Harry tried to look calm, but his hand was trembling as he shook Fletcher's hand. He recognized Fletcher as one of the members of the Purple Gang. Fletcher was clean-shaven and had slicked-back, dark hair and movie-star good looks. He was wearing tight-fitting, expensive leather gloves. Low remembered reading somewhere that Fletcher was a former prizefighter turned bad guy. Low started to turn to get a look at Nicki in the backseat, but stopped when Fletcher started talking.

"We've been watching you for a long time and know you're in tight with the Hiram Walker distillery," Fletcher said. "We want you to work for us getting some of that good Canadian whiskey to our people in Detroit."

Harry's mouth went dry. He nodded and let Fletcher carry on talking.

"We're prepared to front you $80,000 to set this up, $50,000 per load after that."

Nicki leaned forward and put a hand on Harry's shoulder. "The more booze you get stateside, the more money you make. Are you interested?"

The prospect of hundreds of thousands of dollars at his fingertips helped Harry regain his composure.

"This is risky business boys, but I'm glad we've been able to get together this evening. I am definitely your man. But it will take me some time to get things in order. I can get the booze, but I'll have to track down a good boat."

"You've got three weeks, or the deal's off," Fletcher said. "Nicki, give our new Canadian pal the money."

Nicki handed a leather briefcase over the seat to Harry. "There's 80 grand in there, Mr. Low. If you don't come through for us in three weeks, we'll want it back, or we'll hurt your family. You are a family man, aren't you?"

Harry nodded.

"Not to worry boys. This is just going to work out swell," said Harry.

"Our people will be in touch to make the arrangements," Fletcher said. They shook hands, and Harry got out of the car and headed back to Windsor with the briefcase stashed under his seat.

When he got home, he dumped the money on the kitchen table and told his wife about the deal. "I don't want to hear any arguments. If everyone else is getting in on it," Harry said, "I want a piece of the action."

Harry quickly arranged the setup for what would be a multi-million dollar enterprise. By the end of August 1922, Harry Low had closed his pool hall and turned it into a massive storage facility for Canadian Club Whiskey. He was selling bootleg whiskey full time, and it wasn't long before American dollars were piling up in Harry's bank account.

Through his connections on the waterfront, he bought two speedboats and began smuggling booze across the Detroit River. He came up with a clever plan to foil the authorities. He filled out the special customs forms as if the shipment of legal Canadian liquor was going to Cuba or some other tropical port. Of course, he had no intention of sailing that far. Instead, his boats took a short river ride to the Michigan side, where men hired by the Purple Gang unloaded them. Once the boats were empty, they quietly headed back to another dock on the

Canadian side, waited a week and then began the smuggling game all over again.

The Purple Gang was impressed with Low's clever tactics. By appearing to ship the booze to legitimate destinations, Harry was bringing in more booze than the mobsters could ever dream of getting across the border. It wasn't long before the Low-Purple Gang operation was connected to a rum-running network that went from the Windsor docks to Detroit, which in turn supplied underground bars known as "speakeasies" and "blind pigs" in St. Louis, Chicago and Cleveland.

Harry's customs scam was working so well that the Purple Gang demanded more booze. Low was happy to oblige. His one goal in life was to be wealthy, and his dream was quickly becoming a reality. By March 1923, he was known around Windsor as "Dapper Dan," and his headquarters were in the elegant old Canadian Pacific Railway station near the river. He was living the lifestyle of a wealthy gangster and throwing lavish parties. But he wasn't satisfied. He wanted more. So Low decided to expand his operation even further. He started shopping around for bigger boats and a trustworthy crew. It didn't take him long to find exactly what he was looking for.

He turned his attention to cargo ships and bought two—the *Geronimo* and the *Vedas*. The two boats were refurbished World War I minesweepers and patrol boats. The wooden-hulled boats with their wide decks, large hulls and powerful engines had the capacity to carry thousands of cases of booze.

Harry put his background as a mechanic to good use as he overhauled his warships. He even developed special iron drums welded together to encase the powerful engines and act as silencers. His boys could slip back and forth across the foggy river at night invisibly and silently.

The *Vedas* and *Geronimo* sometimes carried Low's booze from Montréal and cast anchor in Lake Erie just outside the 12-mile U.S. territorial limit, where American mobsters' speedboats would race out, unload the cargo and disappear into the foggy night.

But with Low's frequent trips to Canada Customs to complete the forms, the authorities became suspicious. Early one morning the U.S. Coast Guard seized the *Geronimo* as it was being unloaded, tied it up at a Detroit dock and confiscated the booze that remained on board. But it must have been Low's lucky day. A fierce storm blew in and set the *Geronimo* free from its moorings, sending it back to the Canadian side of the Detroit River. Low's men towed it back to harbor and continued their shipments as usual.

Low made so much money so fast that he funneled some of his profits into a luxurious $130,000 mansion in Walkerville, which he built in 1925. It was a replica of an English manor home that he placed in the center of old Walkerville, east of Windsor. Harry loved showing off, and he spared no expense. An ornate gold-tipped fountain decorated one room, and special multipaned windows and hundreds of slate tiles adorned the ceiling in order to recreate the rippled roof of an English country manor.

Low was always coming up with innovative ways to smuggle booze across the border. One night, he put a plan into action that worked better than his wildest dreams. The Windsor Ford plant was closing up for the night, and the workers were streaming out of the factory. They all stopped to watch in amazement when someone yelled and pointed out a truck racing down the hill headed straight for the Detroit River.

"Look out!" a startled worker screamed. "Get out of the way! There's a runaway car!"

A group of men jumped off the road just as a Model T careened wildly down the hill, plunging straight off the dock into the Detroit River. Someone called the Windsor Police, and while the authorities dragged the river looking for bodies, Low and his fellow criminal cohorts quietly loaded three large truckloads of liquor onto the *Vegas*. Fifteen minutes later, the crowd of rubberneckers didn't even notice the old mine-sweeper as she chugged out into to the river headed for the Detroit shore.

But greed eventually spelled the downfall of Dapper Dan. He became reckless in his never-ending quest for more money and power. The police began to keep close tabs on Low and his growing bootlegging empire. Rumors had it that Low tried to bribe RCMP officers and that his associates were linked to a gangland murder. One of their employees, John Allen Kennedy, was discovered bludgeoned and shot through the skull in the woods near the Ohio-Michigan state line. Low was eventually acquitted on murder and bribery charges, but after that he was constantly under surveillance by the police and by the internal revenue service for tax evasion. The strain of Low's legal woes and criminal ties were too much for his wife, and she filed for divorce. It was the beginning of the end for Windsor's Dapper Dan.

Towards the end of Prohibition in 1933, when there was no longer a need for bootleg whiskey in the United States, Low's finances dwindled. He made some bad investments, and by 1938, he was financially crippled. He ended his days on Windsor's seedy Pitt Street with prostitutes, gamblers and the homeless as his companions. Harry Low died penniless and alone in Windsor's Hotel-Dieu Hospital on August 1, 1955.

Harry Low certainly wasn't the only Canadian attracted to the lure of big money that could be made as a bootlegger. Even the smalltime crooks got in on the action. During the height of Prohibition, dozens of speedboats tore across the river, loaded with booze to sell to the Purple Gang.

By 1928, the southern Ontario bootlegging industry became even more violent. Bodies of bootleggers riddled with bullets began washing up on shore, victims of gang hijacking. The public demanded that the police put a stop to the violence.

Booze Busters. Prohibition agents make a public display of dumping confiscated liquor down a city sewer.

The Canadian government tried to crack down on the greedy rumrunners, but the situation was out of control. The Windsor Police spent night after night raiding booze storage sheds along the docks. One October night in 1928, some smalltime Canadian hoods decided that it would be a good idea to hijack one of the liquor storage sheds before the cops got there, but they were too late. The Windsor Police arrived just as the goons were loading up the booze. The red-faced crooks tossed their guns into the water and made a run for it, but they were quickly rounded up and thrown in the local jail.

While Canadian authorities were at least trying to clean up rum-running rackets north of the 49th parallel, it was a different story across the river. Detroit had turned into a bloody war zone between lawmen and gangsters from various organized crime outfits, big and small.

However, the Purple Gang became arrogant, even sloppy to the point where they were terrorizing Detroit with street executions of their enemies, killing a police officer, and in 1930, murdering well-known radio personality Jerry Buckley in front of dozens of witnesses in the lobby of a downtown hotel.

Buckley broadcast to the greater Detroit area each night from the lobby of the LaSalle Hotel. His control booth and microphone were set up in the window of the LaSalle. People walking by on the street could watch Buckley as he pontificated about current events and his opinions on the world. The further he got into his broadcast, the more animated he became, and people came from miles around to watch him flail his arms as he spoke into the microphone. On this particular July evening, he was especially proud of his show. He'd just spent a half-hour calling for the resignation of Detroit Mayor Charles Bowles, condemning Bowles for being soft on the Purple Gang.

"I tell you, Bowles is as crooked as a three-legged dog," Buckley exclaimed to a colleague after the show. "Right after he became mayor, gangland killings doubled, and the speakeasies and gambling dens were doing a roaring business. Tonight, I believe I've brought his career to an end. You should have seen the phone light up!"

An associate of the Purple Gang was listening closely to every word Buckley said on the air. John Mirabella turned red with anger.

"That fat mouthpiece is turning people of Detroit against us." he said. He called up his buddies, Russell Syracuse and Joe English.

"Let's go get him. I know exactly where he's hanging out right now."

Around 12:30 AM, the three men entered the LaSalle Hotel lobby. Buckley was sitting in a wingback chair in the hotel bar talking to a young woman. She had called the radio announcer after his broadcast asking if she could meet to talk about a career in journalism. While Syracuse stood guard in the doorway, Mirabella and English walked up to where Buckley was sitting and stopped directly in front of the stunned announcer. Within seconds, both men pulled out revolvers and emptied them into Buckley. He was killed instantly, with 11 of 12 bullets hitting him in the face and chest. The chair exploded in a mess of blood and stuffing. Less than two hours after signing off from his radio broadcast, Buckley was dead. The assassins ran out of the hotel, across Woodward Avenue and disappeared into the night. No one was ever convicted of the killing.

By 1929, the members of the Purple Gang had become celebrities around Detroit. They made no effort to hide their mobster status. They dined in the finest restaurants, partied at the ritziest nightspots and wore the finest suits. According to one news account, they were known for their "gaudy display of showmanship, calculated to impress their humble neighbors and feed a colossal conceit."

One of the members, Harry Fleisher, drove a 16-cylinder Cadillac with bulletproof windows. He also wore a watch studded with 25 diamonds arranged to form his initials. By the age of 25, Fleisher had compiled an impressive police record that included kidnapping, robbery, counterfeiting and assault. Although a short man (only 5'6"), he had dashing good looks and considered himself a ladies' man. He had a weakness for blonde, buxom women.

Fleisher earned himself a prime spot in the hallowed hall of gangster history in Detroit when he and three other Purple Gang members orchestrated one of Motor City's bloodiest gangland executions, the Collingwood Manor Apartment Massacre. This bullet-riddled event also set in motion the eventual end of the Purple Gang.

A rival group of gangsters called the Sugarhouse Gang had been caught hijacking several of the Purple's booze shipments and skimming from Canadian bootleggers. When they failed to heed repeated warnings to cease their activities, Fleisher ordered his men to find out exactly who was responsible. In less than a week, he had the names and addresses of the culprits. They were 31-year-old Hymie Paul, "Nigger" Joe Lebowitz and 28-year-old Joe "Izzy" Sutker.

These men had been hijacking booze from both friends and enemies, and they had also double-crossed business partners. So after the Purples had repeatedly warned them to pay back the stolen money, they decided it was time for action. The Purples had just bought themselves Thompson submachine guns to add to their growing arsenal, and Harry Fleisher and the boys decided that it was time to put them to the test.

"We're going to put so many holes in these boys, the wind will whistle right through 'em," Fleisher chuckled, as he came up with a plan.

The Purples hired baby-faced Harry Keywell, who was famous for his role in the St. Valentine's Day Massacre in Chicago in 1929, as the machine gunner. Fleisher decided the best strategy to carry out the hit was to arrange a meeting with the Sugarhouse Gang on the premise that the Purples wanted to smooth everything over and wipe the slate clean. He sent a note to the gang's accountant, Solomon "Solly" Levine. The meeting would be held at 1740 Collingwood, Apartment 211, at 3:00 PM on September 16, 1931.

To Hymie, Nigger and Izzy, a peace conference sounded like a good idea. They relaxed and prepared for the meeting, thinking that all was about to be forgiven.

On Tuesday afternoon, September 16, at precisely 3:00 PM, the three men along with Solly arrived at the Collingwood Manor Apartments. They were so certain the meeting was on the level that not one of the four was carrying a gun.

Harry Fleisher met the men at the door of the apartment.

"Harry said he was glad to see us," Levine said later. "Ray Bernstein was sitting at a table eating a bowl of corn flakes, and Irving Milberg and Harry Keywell were there, too. They were fooling around with a record player."

Fleisher looked at Nigger Joe and said, "Which one keeps the books?"

Nigger pointed to Levine, "Four-eyes over there. Best guy with numbers we ever had."

The men sat side by side on the couch; they had a drink and smoked cigars. About 45 minutes later, Bernstein got up and went to the phonograph.

"Wadda ya boys want to hear?" he asked with his back to the room.

That was the cue the triggermen were waiting for. Fleisher jumped to his feet, pulled his .38 revolver out of his shoulder holster and fired two shots pointblank into Nigger Joe's face. The second shot whizzed past Levine's head and blew Joe's head off.

At the same time, Milberg and Keywell fired at Sutker and Hymie Paul. The hail of gunfire caught the trio by surprise. Although they tried to get away, they were no match for Keywell's tommy gun. He sprayed a deadly arc of bullets into the three men.

When the gun smoke cleared, an eerie silence descended on the room. Three gangsters lay dead or dying in a spreading pool of blood. Paul's twisted corpse lay on the floor in front of the couch, eight slugs in his back. Nigger Joe's crumpled body lay in the hallway, and his brains were splattered all over the walls. The killer watched as Izzy, who was barely alive, grunted in shallow breaths as he tried to pull himself by his fingernails along the hardwood floor. He didn't get far. Within a minute he was dead. All three corpses still had cigars clenched in their hands.

Fleisher leaned down asked, "You okay, Four-eyes?"

"All I could do was nod and blink," recalls Levine.

Fleisher, Bernstein and Milburg dropped their handguns into buckets of paint as they ran out the door, ensuring there would be no fingerprints on the pistols. They piled into a waiting black 1930 Buick.

"Where the hell is Keywell?" Bernstein demanded, as they reached the car.

Just then they heard a shot, and seconds later, Keywell came racing to the car, panting heavily.

"I put another bullet into Nigger Joe for good measure," was all he said, as jumped in the backseat. As the men drove away, Keywell smiled and gently caressed the still warm tommy gun cradled in his lap.

The FBI immediately launched an intensive manhunt across Detroit for the killers. They received hundreds of tips, many coming from the neighbors who claimed to have heard and seen the bold daytime execution. They circulated posters around the city stating that the gunmen were wanted "Dead or Alive."

Within 48 hours, the noose tightened around the killers. Around midnight, on Thursday, September 18, the police moved in on an eastside apartment. When they kicked down the door, they found three of the gangsters, Bernstein, Keywell and Milberg, inside playing cards, drinking and smoking cigars. They surrendered without a fight. When police searched the getaway car, they found enough guns and ammunition to start a war.

The police report states, "Found in the car alleged to be Purple Gang's vehicle used in the slaying of three Detroit men were: a .38 special revolver; one .38 Colt army revolver; one .28 automatic pistol; one .45 army auto revolver; one Marland 30-30 rifle; one Winchester .30 rifle; one 12-gauge Winchester pump-gun; and one Remington 12-gauge sawed-off shotgun."

The Detroit police also told reporters that a bag of ammunition was included in the firearms bonanza, as well as a short-wave radio receiver.

With the killings, the Purples became the first criminals in Detroit to use Thompson submachine guns. On further investigation, newspaper reporters counted more than 110 bullet holes in the walls of the Collingwood apartment's living room and hallway.

During the trial, Prosecutor Toy, summarized the case for the jury:

> I hold no brief for the victims and their occupation. This is no defense, however. These men checked their books with bullets and marked off their accounts with blood. They lured the victims to the apartment with promises of partnership and killed them when they were unarmed and helpless.

The jury deliberated for only 90 minutes before finding all three men guilty. As soon as the verdict was announced, pandemonium erupted in the courtroom. The judge pounded his gavel as security guards tried to calm the outraged supporters of the gangsters.

At the sentencing hearing the following week, all three men received life in prison with no chance of parole, to be served in Michigan State Penitentiary in Marquette. Harry Fleisher was never convicted for his role in the Collingwood Massacre. However, he remained a career criminal until he was convicted in 1945 for robbing a gambling house and for conspiring to

Leaders of the notorious Purple Gang (far side of table), Izzy (left) and Ray (right) Bernstein, on trial in Detroit in 1930 for carrying concealed weapons.

꩜

kill a U.S. Senator. He was sent to Alcatraz to serve a life sentence. On October 8, 1965, he was paroled and spent the remainder of his life working as a warehouse manager in Detroit. Fleisher died in May 1978.

After 34 years behind bars, Harry Keywell, a model prisoner, was released on October 21, 1965. He married, lived a quiet law-abiding life and shunned all publicity.

Milberg and Bernstein both died in prison.

Despite the convictions, the other Purple Gang members continued to lead Detroit's underworld for a few more years. But like many other gangster stories, this one ends in tragedy. Sicilian gangs were moving in on the Purples' territory. The Purples learned the hard way that it takes more than muscle to be successful criminals. They lacked the brainpower and organization of these well-organized Mafia syndicates. The remaining leaders of the Purple Gang were systematically and mysteriously executed. In November 1933, the body of Eddie Fletcher, the mobster who'd cut a bootlegging deal with Harry Low, was found in a car on an isolated country road outside Detroit. He'd been shot several times in the face at close range.

But what really signaled the end of the Purple Gang was the abolition of Prohibition. By 1933, politicians, law enforcement and the general public could see that "The Noble Experiment" was doomed.

On April 3, 1933, Michigan became the first state to vote for repeal of the federal Prohibition law. On April 7, Prohibition was officially over in Michigan. There was no longer any need for bootleggers and whiskey smugglers. The millions of dollars in liquid profits that had made the Jewish thugs one of the most feared and powerful gangs in Detroit's history dried up overnight. The Purple Gang's bloody bootlegging dynasty had come to an abrupt end.

CHAPTER FOUR

Rocco Perri,
Canada's Al Capone (1887–1944)

"I don't kill people, they die all by themselves."

–Rocco Perri

ROCCO PERRI, ONE OF THE MOST POWERFUL and fascinating characters in the history of Canadian organized crime, was interviewed by an enthusiastic 24-year-old reporter by the name of Ernest Hemingway who was then working for the *Toronto Daily Star*.

It was the winter of 1923, and Ernest Hemingway and his then-pregnant wife, Hadley, had recently moved to Canada from Europe so that their child could be born in North America where the doctors and hospitals were better. Hemingway had been trying for weeks to cover the notorious mob leader who had the local police running in circles trying to nab Perri on a variety of charges, the most serious being smuggling bootleg booze and running the numbers. When he got the call that the interview was on, Hemingway grabbed his notebook and ran out of the newsroom.

The interview took place in a little Hungarian restaurant at the corner of Yonge and Bloor Streets in Toronto on a gray January afternoon. Over bowls of onion dumpling soup, smoked sausages and coffee, Hemingway began asking questions. He wanted to find out about Perri's rum-running operation and betting system in southern Ontario. About 10,000 people in Toronto alone used Rocco's bookmakers, playing about $100,000 a day. Rocco eluded the young reporter's questions about his gambling, prostitution and narcotics operations until Hemingway asked about Perri's involvement in a gangland style execution in Hamilton involving two rival bootlegger thugs, Joseph Boytovich and Fred Genessee, who were trying to move in on his turf.

"Hey, I never killed nobody. I hate violence," he told Hemingway. "All I do is run a few numbers and make good whiskey for the thirsty folks."

With that he openly admitted to being the king of bootlegging, but denied any involvement in the deaths of Boytovich and Genessee. The statement would come back to haunt the mob boss years later. Rocco, like many high-profile gangsters, enjoyed basking in the media spotlight. He made the mistake that was so typical of a powerful and successful mob boss: Rocco forgot that he was Public Enemy Number One in Canada.

Rocco Perri was called "Canada's King of the Bootleggers" and "Canada's Al Capone." He was the head of the Calabrian mob, based in Hamilton, Ontario, during the '20s and '30s. He was 5'9" with a stocky build, and it was rumored that he once snapped a man's neck with his powerful hands in a dispute over a baseball score. His voice was his strongest feature, deep and loud, and he would use it assertively when barking out a command.

His partner in crime was his common-law Jewish wife, Bessie Starkman. Mob wives usually exist in a state of denial. To the outside world, these women swear that their husbands are not bloodthirsty outlaws and killers. Instead, they prefer to believe that their men are unfairly harassed by the law

Rocco Perri (1887–1944), the Hamilton gangster called the "King of the Bootleggers," was the first major Mafia figure in Canada.

~×~

because of their Italian background. Expensive clothes, fancy cars and luxurious houses ensure that the women follow the code of silence. But Bessie never denied Rocco's activities; she knew exactly what her husband did for a living. And instead of taking a backseat to her husband's mob dealings, Bessie controlled many of the business decisions and eventually spearheaded the Calabrian mob's international narcotics trade.

The couple's relationship was one of the strangest in the macho, bloodthirsty world of organized crime. Together they became the king and queen of the Canadian underworld. During Prohibition in Ontario, which began south of the border as "The Noble Experiment," Rocco and Bessie created a booze empire that stretched into the United States. While other mobsters shipped liquor by boat along the coast, Rocco used the rail system to smuggle booze into the U.S. for powerful mob bosses, such as Lucky Luciano and Al Capone. His boxcars of illegal booze went to New York, Philadelphia and as far west as Chicago.

Like Capone, Perri developed a huge network of corrupt Canadian power, including judges, politicians and police officers, who looked the other way whenever the Calabrian mob shipped booze and narcotics.

Rocco Perri was born into poverty in the tiny village of Plati, in the Calabrian region in southern Italy, on December 30, 1887. Many of the families in Plati couldn't afford an education for their children, but Rocco's mother convinced the local priest to teach her boy how to read and write. That made him popular with many of the uneducated immigrants when Rocco, age 16, and his family came to Massena, New York.

The Perri family moved to Canada in 1908, and Rocco picked up whatever work he could get; most of it was manual labor. He signed on as a construction worker in Trenton, Ontario, and sweated it out in a rock quarry near Parry Sound. He was even employed by the Canadian National Railway for six months.

In May 1912, Rocco was living in the Little Italy area of Toronto at the corner of Dufferin and St. Claire. He had a falling out with his landlord over arguments with the other tenants and was forced to look for a new place to live. On a day off from his construction job, he decided to follow up on an advertisement in the *Toronto Daily Star*.

Room and board was available at a house in an area known as The Ward, near Dundas and Chestnut Streets. He got off the streetcar at Dundas and walked the three blocks to the rooming house. A striking woman with sparkling blue eyes opened the door. She introduced herself as Bessie Starkman. If there was ever any truth to the cliché love at first sight, this was it. And the feeling was mutual for Bessie, a slight woman with a pale complexion and dark hair. This dapper foreigner with the romantic accent standing in front of her with his tattered old suitcase intrigued Bessie. She was a bored housewife with a husband and two childern, and she was fed up with living in poverty. Rocco moved in and became part of the family, eating meals with them, playing with the kids and helping Bessie's husband Harry with the yard work.

It wasn't long before Bessie and Rocco began a complicated, passionate love affair. As soon as her husband left for work at the bakery, and the children, Lily and Gertrude, were off to school in the morning, Bessie and Rocco were in each other's arms. Within three months, the two lovebirds ran away to find a new life together.

They took the train to St. Catharines, 180 kilometers south of Toronto. The couple was poor. Everything they owned was in a battered old suitcase. Rocco got a job working construction, and Bessie went to work in a bakery. The couple had a son in 1914, but the boy died two days after birth. Within a few years, they had saved some money, and they moved to Hamilton, where they opened up a small corner grocery store on Hess Street in Little Italy.

But Rocco was hungry for more. He wanted wealth and power. When Prohibition was introduced in 1916 in Ontario, it wasn't long before Rocco and Bessie were selling bootleg whiskey at 50 cents a glass. In the basement, Rocco built a simple still the same way his father had back in Italy. The couple used potato peelings as the base for the mash, and they were soon making more than 200 gallons of whiskey per week. When word got around that you could get a glass of whiskey and do your grocery shopping at the same time, the little corner grocery store on Hess Street became a popular place where men could talk politics and the latest sports scores while their wives did the grocery shopping. Bessie set up a little bar in the back, and business became so good that often the neighboring set of elbows leaning on the bar were attached to a politician, judge or high-profile businessman. The Closed sign on the grocery store went up at 6:00 PM, and the parties lasted well into the night.

Perri's Hamilton was a tough, blue-collar steel town, as it still is today. Located at the western end of Lake Ontario, the town was perfectly suited to the Calabrian mob's cross-border trade. The Calabrian mob, or "The Ndrangheta," originated in the Calabrian region of southern Italy where Rocco was born. As thousands of Italian immigrants came to Canada from Italy in the early years of the 20th century, a small number brought with them the Mafia customs of the Calabrian mob. By 1920, the Calabrian mob controlled crime in Canada, and Rocco Perri turned the secret society into the greatest criminal organization Canada has ever seen.

Rocco's gregarious nature made him a favorite among young and old, rich and poor on Hamilton's streets. He could charm family and friends and then exploit them for his own greed, and it wasn't long before he had several family members and friends running similar "grocery stores" throughout Hamilton. In those days, Rocco answered to no one and had no competition for the profits. Within a few short years, Rocco was the most powerful mob boss and rumrunner in eastern Canada.

Just four years after their move to Hamilton, life was different for the enterprising young couple. Rocco wore pinstriped suits, starched shirts and diamond stickpins. He was a big tipper, and was always seen with a cigarette in a trademark silver holder dangling from his mouth. It wasn't uncommon for him to spend an hour each day with his barber.

Bessie, too, dressed in the height of fashion. She always wore the finest dresses adorned with diamonds. The couple bought a luxurious house on Bay Street South near downtown Hamilton, and they were often seen at the racetrack. By the mid-1920s, Rocco and Bessie were local celebrities, rubbing elbows with the upper crust and holding lavish parties at their opulent home.

In business and in life, timing is everything. Although Ontario had outlawed the retail sale of liquor, the federal government approved and licensed distilleries and breweries to produce and export. In 1919, the Calabrian mob owned 23 breweries in Ontario. And Rocco had a plan. His successful Mafia operation connected him to his "family" counterparts south of the border, such as "Lucky" Luciano, who had a stranglehold on the organization in New York City. The two men set up an operation to smuggle Canadian whiskey into the U.S.

Luciano's reputation as a ruthless gang leader was the result of his being a founding member of the notorious Five Points Gang and being named by police as the prime suspect in several murders. From 1895 to 1917, this vicious gang of young thugs operated in the Five Points district in Manhattan's Lower East Side.

By 1920, Lucky Luciano was at the top of his game in the bootlegging rackets and had become the most powerful member of the New York Mafia. He'd earned his nickname for his ability to pick winning horses at the track, and like Rocco Perri, was a dandy dresser. He was often seen in the popular nightclubs on Broadway, looking menacing because of the evil droop to his right eye that was caused by an ugly scar he got in a knife fight.

Luciano was well versed in the smuggling game, and with his Canadian cohort, Rocco Perri, soon controlled the Ontario distilleries and all the trucks shipping booze to New York from Canada. The two gangs flourished financially, generating millions of dollars in the bootlegging business. With the growing demand for more liquor from south of the border, Rocco quickly expanded his smuggling operations from Montréal to Windsor. The Calabrian mob used every creative method they could to get the moonshine flowing from Ontario and Québec into the underground bars, called speakeasies, south of the border. False floorboards in cars, second gas tanks and hidden compartments got the booze past the prying eyes of customs agents.

It didn't hurt that Rocco and Bessie had a built-in clientele. World War I ended in 1918, and the boys were coming home. After months of fighting the bloodiest war in history, the young Canadian veterans were not impressed with Prohibition. They were ready to let loose and celebrate, and Rocco Perri made sure they were never thirsty. To get liquor, all a fella had to do was pick up the phone and call one of Rocco's bootleggers or visit one of his numerous speakeasies that thrived in the Ontario underground.

Rocco also began bribing the police to keep quiet about the Calabrian mob's smuggling operations. But unlike his U.S. counterparts, Rocco always insisted that he disliked violence, and he took pride in running his organization without the bloodshed of his American colleagues. That was until November 12, 1923, when bullets began to fly, and blood flowed in the streets of Hamilton. A double murder shocked the city and got the bootleg wars off to a bloody start. The brutal gangland execution shone the media spotlight on Rocco's operation and set the law on his tail.

Two smalltime crooks, "Big" Joe Boytovich and Fred Genessee, arrived in Steel Town in October. They'd heard the booze business was thriving in Hamilton, so they decided to set up their own bootlegging operation. But instead of running a standard homebrew operation with grain mash, Big Joe and Fred came up with an innovative plan to make whiskey cheaper and quicker than with the conventional method.

Big Joe earned his nickname simply enough. He was 6'5" and weighed 350 pounds. He talked and moved slowly, but he was actually a highly educated man. He knew several languages, including Latin, which he'd learned while studying to be a priest. Fred Genessee, on the other hand, was a small man, standing 5'2" and weighing only 120 pounds. He may have been slight of build, but he had a ferocious temper and was a man not to be crossed.

The two hoodlums had heard that Rocco ruled his turf with diplomacy rather than violence and had convinced themselves that the Calabrian mob boss wouldn't give them any trouble. They couldn't have been more wrong.

Fred and Big Joe made a deal with a Detroit undertaker to ship rubbing alcohol in five-gallon cans at one dollar per unit. Rubbing alcohol differed from regular drinking alcohol only in that it contained a denaturant, making it unfit to drink. No U.S. excise tax was levied on rubbing alcohol, so the boys could ship it a ton at a time by rail. On a farm east of town, the bootlegging entrepreneurs would then run the fluid through their still to clean it up, leaving drinkable alcohol ready for sale as vodka or gin. In order to turn it into whiskey, all that was needed was a little food coloring. It was a brilliant and profitable idea. They were turning $1-a-gallon rubbing alcohol into $25-a-gallon booze.

When Rocco heard of Joe and Fred's operation, he flew into a rage and slammed the table with his fist. "I want those arrogant bastards taught a lesson," he screamed at his startled men. "I want them dead."

He ordered two of his top triggermen to do the job. Thomas Jacobitvh and Howard Gallop were World War I veterans.

A Prohibition agent examines a confiscated still. High-test liquor was brewed illegally in copper stills by moonshiners. The recipe (often handed down from father to son) was a closely guarded secret. A typical batch of white lightning contained a sack of corn meal or cattle molasses, 100 gallons of water, 10 pounds of yeast and 100 pounds of sugar. The ingredients were mixed together in a large crock or barrel and left to ferment. The "mash" was then heated to the point of vaporization in a copper kettle. The vapor was siphoned off into another container through coiled copper tubing. The resulting condensation was moonshine. The mash was usually used again to brew more batches. If the moonshine passed the "taste" test—burning in a spoon with a bright blue flame—it was ready to be bottled and sold.

They'd fought together in some of the bloodiest battles in France—Hill 76, Vimy Ridge and Passchendaele. Jacobitvh was a decorated marksman and sniper, having been awarded the French Croix de Guerre for bravery. Gallop was wounded twice and suffered lung damage in a poison gas attack.

But the war years had given the two a taste for blood and a talent for killing. When they came home to Ontario after the war, the prospect of going back to mundane jobs bored them. They met Rocco at one of his grocery store/bars and began working for him. Their primary job was to deliver bootleg booze to customers and collect the money, so planning a cold-blooded, orchestrated murder was something new. The two gangsters took on the mission with enthusiasm.

Thomas and Howie quickly discovered that their quarry followed the same pattern day after day. They'd leave their apartments in the Queen's Hotel each morning and have breakfast at the Pacific Cafe on King Street.

"They come out of the hotel at the same time every day," Thomas said. "These guys are so predictable, this hit will be as easy as shooting fish in a barrel."

But Howie wasn't convinced the executions were going to be that easy. The gunmen had no escape route, no hot getaway car and no plan. Their intended victims left the hotel at the same time each day, but it was at 11:00 AM, and the hotel was on a busy street.

"We can't just pull up and gun them down in broad daylight," Howard said.

"I agree," said Thomas. "So that's why we'll kidnap 'em first, take them out of town and then whack 'em."

So it was on Tuesday morning, November 19, that the two gunmen pulled up to the Queen's Hotel in a black 1919 Studebaker. A fierce winter storm was pounding Hamilton, and the two men sat shivering in their car as they waited for Boytovich and Genessee to exit the hotel. They didn't have long to wait.

Fred and Joe sauntered out of the hotel, pausing to flip up their collars against the frigid wind and snow.

"There they are. Let's go," Tom said.

Howie was the first out of the car, pistol in hand. He walked quickly up to the two men, as Tom opened the door and got out. Howie stuck the gun under Big Joe's nose, grabbed Frank's arm in a vice-like grip and quietly ordered both men into the backseat of the Studebaker. Tom had the back door open and was standing to the side with a submachine gun on his hip pointed at the two surprised and frightened men.

"Get the hell inside, right now," Tom muttered. Howie took the machine gun from Tom and leveled it at both men who were hunched over in the backseat while Tom got behind the wheel. Howie slammed the door behind them and jumped into the passenger seat. Tom slammed the gas pedal down, and they sped away. The kidnapping had taken less than a minute.

Howie kept the machine gun trained on the two lying in the back on the floor as Tom wheeled the Studebaker down King Street to an old warehouse on the south side of town. They roughly hauled the two into the building, blindfolded, bound and gagged them and left them lying on the floor. Howie and Tom drank whiskey, smoked cigarettes and played cards until nightfall. Every now and then one of the hostages would moan or roll over, and Howie would give him a sharp kick in the ribs to silence him. Rocco arrived just after 9:00 PM. He walked into the warehouse, nodded to his two boys and then turned his attention to Joe and Fred.

He kneeled down and pulled Joe's head up by the hair and snarled, "You were warned about selling booze on my turf. I don't like greedy little pigeons."

He dropped Joe's head with a sickening thud on the concrete floor. He stood up and stomped on Joe's chest hard three times, five times. Howie and Tom lost count. Joe let out an eerie moan through the gag and passed out. Rocco then turned to Fred and ripped off the blindfold. Grabbing him by the hair, he yanked Fred's head up until it was inches from his face and stared into the terrified man's eyes.

Then, with a look of disgust, Rocco began punching the hoodlum until his face was a bloody pulp. Sweating, Rocco stood up and looked over at Howie and Tom.

"Take these two out and whack 'em," he said, as he wiped his bloody hands on a rag. "But don't hide the bodies. I want them found as a sign to everybody else not to mess with me."

An hour after Rocco left, Tom and Howie checked outside to see if it was all clear and then hauled the two battered men back into the Studebaker. Tom drove southeast out of town in the snowstorm for about 40 minutes. He stopped by the old stone bridge at Albion Mills. It was just after midnight, and not a soul was around. Howie pulled Joe out of the car by his feet and dragged him to the base of the bridge. He propped Joe up on his knees, hands still tied behind his back, his head leaning against the stone. Howie took out his .45, and without hesitation, shot Big Joe once in the back of the neck. The blast nearly ripped Joe's head from his body. Howie got back in the car, and Tom wheeled back onto the road. Howie noticed that Fred wasn't making a sound. Tom had knocked him out because Fred had gone berserk when he heard the gunshot.

They drove for another 15 minutes and stopped at Stony Creek. This time it took both men to drag Fred's unconscious body to a spot under a cliff by the creek.

"He's not even going to know what hit him," Tom grunted, as he looked down at the body.

He cocked the submachine gun and sprayed a quick burst into Fred's torso and face. The bullets tore apart the left side of his belly and his face under his right eye through to his left cheek. The two gangsters quickly jumped back into their car and drove back to Hamilton to tell the boss that the job was finished.

Early the next morning, a milkman found the nearly head-less body of Joseph Boytovich at the base of the bridge in Albion Mills. Some children playing hooky found the bullet-riddled body of Fred Genessee at Stony Creek. Within hours, news of the gangland executions had southern Ontario abuzz. By 10:00 AM, Hamilton Police Chief Robert Whatley and his men were on the scene.

The 45-year-old police chief was a familiar sight around the streets of Steel Town. He was often seen striding down James Street for his midday walk, carrying an ebony cane with a silver handle. At 6'3", with a handlebar mustache and military appearance, he was a forbidding figure. His army past was well known. At the age of 20, he had served in South Africa, fighting in the Boer War with the Cape Mounted Police.

When the war was over, he moved to Ontario, where he enlisted in the Canadian army. He was a lieutenant with the 23rd Northern Pioneers and based at Parry Sound. In 1907, he married local schoolteacher Annie Nicolson, and the couple had four daughters. Three years later, the city of Hamilton hired Whatley as Deputy Police Chief, and promoted him to chief in 1915 when Chief Alexander Smith died.

Chief Whatley was familiar with the Calabrian mob's criminal activities, but mostly they kept him busy busting ragtag moonshiners. Rocco and his boys had the police chief running. The tires on their police cruisers were bald trying to catch the mob smuggling whiskey. In Whatley's first six months in office, the Hamilton Police located and destroyed nine of Rocco and Bessie's moonshine stills. So much bootlegged liquor was confiscated that the chief began using it as antifreeze in the radiators of police department vehicles.

Whatley was one of the first police chiefs in Canada to arrange his city into divisions by splitting up the force. He was also successful in shutting down many of Rocco's gambling rackets and whorehouses. His high success rate was due in part to his clever use of out-of-town cops to work under-cover in Hamilton.

But somehow, Rocco managed to stay one step ahead of the police chief and his men. It was the little fish that the Hamilton Police were sending to the slammer, not the big ones. The wily mob boss had several trucks and boats in his growing empire, and he always used trusted men to do his smuggling. Rocco was shrewd and cunning, making certain he was never on the scene when a bust went down.

The murder investigation in November 1923 was new to Chief Whatley. As Whatley's detectives poured over the crime scene, it was all too obvious that it was a mob hit. The two men had been savagely beaten and tortured before they were shot. But the spent cartridges from a submachine gun at Stony Creek and the one .45 casing at Albion Mills were the only clues the Hamilton Police Department had to go on.

Whatley had seen this coming for a long time. Rocco had ruled criminal activity in Hamilton with an iron hand for years. But times were changing, and more criminals were moving in on Rocco's turf. He realized that Rocco had done what he had to do in order to control his turf, but the problem was finding the evidence to support his theory. And no evidence existed unless someone ratted out the Calabrian mob boss. That was Whatley's only hope. As he stood by the river watching Fred Genessee's body being carted away to the morgue, he knew it would be difficult to prove that Rocco was behind the murders.

On November 19, Whatley brought Perri to police head-quarters for questioning, but the mob boss denied any involve-ment in the brutal murders. With no evidence, Rocco walked out of the Hamilton Police Station a free man.

To this day, no one has been convicted in the killings of Genessee and Boytovich. Police Chief Whatley took the unsolved case to his grave. He died in his house on Flatt

Avenue a few months later after losing his battle with pneumonia and pleurisy. He was just 46 years old.

It was that same winter; Ernest Hemingway interviewed Perri for the *Toronto Daily Star* at the Hungarian restaurant at the corner of Bloor and Yonge Streets. In typical gangster hubris, Rocco hoped to set the record straight and show the world that he wasn't such a bad guy with the famous quote: "Hey, I never killed nobody. I hate violence. All I do is run a few numbers and make good whiskey for the thirsty folks."

In 1928, a Royal Commission investigation into Rocco's bootlegging during Prohibition used his statement in the Hemingway interview against him. He told the commission that he was just a successful businessman who'd made his money as a pasta salesman delivering his product from door to door. But the commission wasn't buying it, especially after reading Hemingway's article. Maybe it was because Perri made $780,000 that year. Or perhaps it was that investigators found eight fat bank accounts in his wife's name. One showed that she'd deposited more than $900,000 at once. He was sentenced to six months in jail for perjury.

While Rocco was in prison, his wife and partner in crime took control of the Calabrian mob. From rum-running to gambling rackets, Bessie took care of all facets of the gang's criminal activities. With Rocco's approval, she even expanded their Hamilton-based racket into a multi-million dollar international cocaine, heroin and morphine business.

Prohibition not only set the stage for bootleg booze, but it also created a demand for narcotics. If people couldn't get a drink during the Roaring Twenties, some switched to cocaine, opium and marijuana to get high. Bessie made sure her customers were well supplied. The distribution of these illicit substances became extremely profitable for the gangster underworld. Using the mob's connections in New York, Philadelphia and Chicago to buy and sell the drugs, she was

Bessie Starkman (1889–1930), Rocco Perri's common-law wife and partner in crime. Bessie was the only Jewish woman in history to command an Italian mob.

now pulling in more than a quarter of a million dollars a week for the Calabrian mob.

When Rocco got out of jail, he was so impressed with Bessie's narcotics operation that he gave her complete control of the mob's drug trade and finances. But his wife's arrogance and drive soon began to cause tension in the underworld in Ontario. Other mob leaders and gang members were angered that Rocco would give a woman such a high position of power and hand over control of such wealth. They also resented that Bessie ran her part of the racket and the gang finances with a firm hand and didn't allow for any profit sharing among other Calabrian gangsters working in Toronto, Ottawa and Montréal. Machismo permeated the male-dominated Italian underworld; a woman should stay at home and be a quiet wife and a good mother, not a Mafia boss.

The gangster couple made a lot of enemies in a short period of time, and it wasn't long before trouble was brewing in the Hamilton underworld for Rocco and Bessie. As more gangs moved in for a bigger slice of the gambling, prostitution and narcotic rackets, violence erupted. The first sign of a gang war to oust Rocco Perri from power occurred in the summer of 1930, and it was Bessie Starkman who paid the ultimate price.

The couple arrived home at about 11:00 PM from a party at Rocco's cousin's house north of Hamilton. Both were drunk, and as Rocco fumbled with the backdoor key, Bessie was getting out of the car in the garage. Just as Rocco turned the key, a shotgun blast tore through the darkness. Seconds later, another blast exploded in the night. Bessie fell to the ground; two shotgun blasts had ripped into her tiny frame. Rocco ran to his dying wife's side as the hired assassin slipped away into the overcast Hamilton night. When police arrived 15 minutes later, they found the tough mob boss kneeling in a pool of blood and holding his common-law wife of nine years, sobbing and kissing her hair. Police reports from the time say that she was dead before she hit the ground.

Rocco went out of his mind with grief, offering a $5000 reward for information leading to the killer. But the gang war for criminal supremacy of the streets was on, and any would-be informants may have been too afraid for their own lives to come forward.

One of the prime suspects was triggerman Tony Mortoni, hired killer and vicious thug, also known as Crazy Boy. He was a slender, cunning eccentric who was known to eat raw liver spread thickly on soda crackers and washed down with Orange Crush. When he was going about his dirty deeds, he liked to disguise himself with a cheesy, dime-store mustache. He'd experimented with various methods of killing—shooting, stabbing, beating, poisoning, bombing—but the police couldn't pin Bessie's brutal murder on Crazy Boy. He was detained by the police and released after several hours of intense but pointless interrogation. The murder was never solved. Some say the real target was Rocco himself.

The grief-stricken mobster held a lavish funeral for the love of his life. He buried her in a $3000 silver-trimmed casket. Around her neck was the $10,000 diamond necklace she'd worn on the night she was murdered. The *Hamilton Spectator* reported that the hearse was covered in white flowers. Fifteen cars followed the funeral procession through Hamilton, as thousands of men and women dressed in black lined the streets to pay their respects to the Perri Gang.

Although Rocco Perri had the support of many Hamiltonians, Bessie's death marked the beginning of the end for the ruthless gangster, although he did manage to avoid any serious jail time. Even in 1932, when police busted two of his bootleg stills in a house on Concession Street, his goons took the heat. That bust took more than 26,000 gallons of illegal whiskey off the market, but within a month, Rocco had four more stills in operation.

After Bessie's death, the determination and drive that had made him "Canada 's Al Capone" began to fade. Now in his mid-forties, Rocco found comfort in the arms of another strong Jewish woman named Annie Newman. She tried to help Rocco run his narcotics and gambling rackets, but without Bessie's lust for power, financial expertise and gangland contacts, cracks began to appear in Rocco's mob empire.

During the early '30s, bootlegging was still bringing millions of dollars into the Calabrian mob's coffers, but Rocco was losing respect among his gang members. There were now too many rival gangs moving into his territory for him to even attempt to defend his turf, and he was losing control of his troops. A mob boss must be respected, feared and honored by his men to become a powerful and successful leader. But now, there was talk among his henchmen that Perri had "gone soft" after Bessie's death and that he'd lost the will to fight. Many of his most trusted confidantes and triggermen turned their backs on Perri in disgust and went to work for other Sicilian gangs working in southern Ontario.

But there were more darkling shadows looming for Canada's King of the Bootleggers and his outlaw empire. South of the border, the American people were demanding an end to "The Noble Experiment." U.S. lawmakers realized that Prohibition was a miserable failure, and it came to an end officially on December 5, 1933. Rocco Perri's bootlegging days were over. Overnight, he lost millions of dollars in revenue from his smuggling operations. For the next few years, he managed to profit from gambling, prostitution and narcotics, but the amount of money was nowhere near what he'd made smuggling booze.

Not only was Rocco's criminal and financial livelihood slipping away from him, he also began to fear for his life. The vicious Sicilian gangs that were now controlling most of Ontario's narcotics and gambling operations wanted the aging kingpin dead.

Two attempts were made on Perri's life. On March 20, 1938, his front porch was blown to pieces by dynamite. Fortunately, Rocco wasn't home at the time. Then, on November 23 that same year, a bomb went off just as he got into his car outside the Tivoli Restaurant on James Street. He was thrown clear by the blast and only suffered a few bruises, but two of his friends were seriously injured. So, the man who was once treated like a celebrity in his beloved Hamilton couldn't even walk down the street without looking over his shoulder.

But it was a bizarre twist of turn of events at the beginning of World War II that brought the legacy of Canada's Public Enemy Number One to an end. In 1940, Rocco was arrested by Canadian lawman Frank Zaneth. Tough, wiry and clever, the 50-year-old Zaneth was one of the RCMP's first secret agents assigned to a small elite team whose mission was to investigate Canadian mobs. In his reports, he was known only as "Operative Number One." As a member of the elite group, he would often don disguises as he went undercover to infiltrate the gangster underworld.

The Mountie's top undercover agent hounded and tracked the slippery gangster throughout his career. He finally got his man in 1940, when he arrested Perri in a gambling den in Hamilton. But it wasn't the notorious gangster's mob dealings that led to his capture. Instead, Zaneth arrested Rocco under the War Measures Act because of Perri's Italian ancestry.

So in 1940, Canada's King of the Bootleggers ended up in a jail cell in Petawawa, Ontario, as an enemy of Canada along with thousands of other Italian Canadians. After Italy declared war on the Allied Nations on June 10, 1940, Italians from all walks of life—shopkeepers, factory workers and doctors from Ontario, Québec and Nova Scotia—were put on a train to Petawawa and treated as prisoners of war.

When Rocco was freed in 1943, he worked at several low-profile jobs in Toronto, even as a janitor and usher at a Dundas movie theater. But he longed for the old days; he wanted his power and money back. Returning to Hamilton, he renewed old connections and tried, without success, to conduct mob business once again. The return of the old-style gangster was looked on as more of a joke than a threat by the heads of other criminal operations. The gray-haired gangster was seen more as a comic figure in the underworld rather than a ruthless killer. Nonetheless, someone must have sensed the aging godfather could still be a threat to mob business.

On April 23, 1944, 57-year-old Perri was visiting his cousin Joseph Sergi north of Hamilton for Sunday dinner. It had been a nice evening, but Rocco wasn't feeling well and complained of a headache. At about 9:30 PM, he pushed his chair back and stood up from the table.

"My head feels like it's going to split open," he said, rubbing his temples. "I'm going outside for some air."

He put on his hat and coat and went out the front door. Rocco Perri never came back. By 11:30, Sergi and his brother were pacing the floor, wondering what had happened to the old man. Together, they searched the neighborhood, banging on doors and asking if anyone had seen Perri. The answer in the quiet neighborhood was always the same, "Sorry, we've heard nothing."

The next morning, Joseph Sergi called the police to report that the 57-year-old gangster had vanished mysteriously. The news of the missing mobster hit front-page news across Canada, and radio stations broadcast the news across the country. But the story soon faded away. In the weeks and months and years to come, nothing was ever heard of Rocco Perri. The case of his disappearance was never solved. After he walked out of his cousin's house that April night, Rocco Perri was never seen again. Some say he fled to Acapulco where he changed his name and lived to be an old man in his 80s. Others still believe that he is buried in cement in a 45-gallon drum at the bottom of Hamilton Bay.

CHAPTER FIVE

Rum Row
(1920–1933)

"Man, that's good booze....Burns like
fire down my throat."

–a Chicago customer

ON A WARM AND SUNNY JULY AFTERNOON in 1923, the docks on
the islands of St. Pierre and Miquelon, located 16 miles southwest of Newfoundland, are crowded with people. Men, women
and children cheerfully help each other haul heavy wooden
cases up the gangplank and onto the decks of two schooners
tied up on either side of the dock. Sixteen deckhands sing sea
songs as they gently pass the cases down the line to the hold
below. Children giggle and sing along. Hundreds of cases are
stacked in neat rows in the belly of the ship. The cargo is fragile
and worth a fortune to the islanders. Inside the cases are bottles
of high-quality Canadian whiskey illegally bound for the
United States.

This was a typical scene in harbors along the coastline of
Canada's Atlantic provinces during Prohibition. The area
became known as Rum Row. From 1920 to 1933, almost every
coastal community from Newfoundland to Nova Scotia played
a major role in the trafficking of alcohol during the Prohibition

era in the United States. The Atlantic provinces were once a place of mystery and murder, booze, bloodshed and sinister gangster deals. The hundreds of islands and coves around Nova Scotia offered ideal hiding places for boats loaded with illegal liquor.

Smuggling boatloads of booze into the U.S. was a dangerous and sometimes deadly livelihood, but many maritime families took the risk and it sustained them through the tough economic times of the '20s and '30s. The precise profits will no doubt never be known because the rumrunners often exaggerated their income from bootlegging. But to this day, many prominent Nova Scotia families can attribute their wealth to the sale of liquid gold.

One thing is clear; enormous profits were made. Dark rum or whiskey could be purchased for as little as 40 cents per gallon and then sold on the black market for $4.00 per gallon. The American gangsters would bottle it and label the booze using counterfeit labels. Al Capone did just that with his "Old Log Cabin" brand.

The movement for the prohibition of alcohol began in the early 20th century, when Americans who were concerned about the adverse effects of drinking began forming temperance organizations. These groups became powerful political forces, calling for total national abstinence to improve the health of Americans and the country's moral fiber.

On January 16, 1919, the U.S. government ratified the National Prohibition Act, commonly known as the Volstead Act. A year later on January 16, 1920, the manufacture, sale, or transportation of intoxicating liquors became law. Prohibition became known as "The Noble Experiment."

Section 3 of the Act states: "No person shall on or after the date when the eighteenth amendment to the Constitution of the United States goes into effect, manufacture, sell, barter, transport, import, export, deliver, furnish or possess any intoxicating liquor except as authorized in this Act, and all the provisions of this Act shall be liberally construed to the end that the use of intoxicating liquor as a beverage may be prevented."

Overnight, America became officially dry. Or did it? As soon as the U.S. enacted Prohibition, the American underworld began making plans to smuggle whiskey from Canada into the United States. The coastlines and land borders of the United States offered an 18,700-mile invitation to smugglers, and the era of rum-running and whiskey smuggling was born. Fueled by ruthless gangsters competing against one another for territory and profits, Prohibition ushered in a lawlessness America had never seen before. Gangsters set up smuggling rackets from Newfoundland to New Orleans. Canadian rum ships snuck into American waters loaded with booze. The cargo was then transferred to the mob's fast motorboats, which then transported the cases of liquor to shore and loaded it onto trucks to be taken inland to secret warehouses. The underworld bribed dock workers and sea captains to look the other way when freighters brought in cases of contraband Canadian whiskey mixed among cases of perfectly legal and properly labeled commodities such as flour, sugar and many other household goods.

It was during this time that the French islands of St. Pierre and Miquelon, 16 miles off the southern coast of Newfoundland, became a smuggler's paradise for the American gangsters and Canadian rumrunners. After their discovery by the Portuguese in 1520, French navigator and explorer Jacques Cartier claimed the islands for his homeland in 1535. Many early residents of the territory were of Basque and Breton origin and made their living from the sea. As a result of the booming fishing trade, Britain and France quarreled over St. Pierre for many years until 1763, when the Treaty of Paris permanently awarded the islands to France.

Until Prohibition in 1920, the economy of these small islands had been based on cod fishing for more than a century. The fish were caught, dried and then shipped all over the world.

But between 1920 and 1933, the storing and shipping of whiskey and rum became the mainstay of the island's economy. When American mobsters discovered that the remote location of the islands was an ideal base for smuggling, they set up warehouses to hold enormous stocks of whiskey distilled in Canada that were legally exported from Canada to St. Pierre and Miquelon.

Much of the high-quality Canadian whiskey and rum came via the St. Lawrence Seaway from the Bronfman's distillery in Montréal, Québec or Hiram Walker's near Windsor, Ontario. Canadian distillers made millions of dollars from the American mobsters during this era. U.S. gangsters such as Lucky Luciano in New York and Al Capone in Chicago purchased up to 300,000 cases per month from the St. Pierre facility. Capone even visited the islands to ensure that his own operation was running smoothly.

In the 1920s, almost the entire population of the islands made its living from bootlegged booze. Many of the local folk made a much better living maintaining the booze warehouses or working on the docks loading liquor onto the ships than they ever did from cod fishing.

In most homes in other provinces plants and flowers adorned the windows, but on St. Pierre folks had bottles of rum, whiskey and cigarettes on display. Everything was for sale. Many of the houses that were built during this time were constructed of wood from the empty whiskey crates that piled up near the docks. Most looked as if no one had ever painted them.

The rum-running captains liked St. Pierre harbor, a snug little cove with one narrow side that was difficult to navigate into if the wind was blowing hard. But the smugglers appreciated the setup; it offered safe haven from the sea and from the law.

American mobsters would often visit the islands to check up on their operations. The islanders invited the gangsters to the warehouses where the liquor was stored and allowed them to see the wide variety of blends of whiskey and rum stored in casks in row upon row of long wooden cradles. The owners of the warehouses also allowed prospective buyers to sample the liquor using long, enamel dippers. Teacher's Highland Cream was a favorite among the U.S. gangsters. Other favorite brands were Sandy McNabb and White Horse.

Rum also came in from the West Indies where the finest grade was made from molasses from sugar cane. It sold for 25 cents per cup in St. Pierre in the little shops on Main Street, but mobsters preferred good Canadian whiskey to Caribbean rum. The rum was often thick and greasy—turn an emptied glass over, and an oily film from the dregs would slide slowly down the surface.

But the islands of St. Pierre and Miquelon weren't the only locations along Rum Row doing a lucrative business selling booze to the American mobsters. Some of the hooch for sale was just plain, old-fashioned moonshine. Some of the best white lightning was cooked up in the Nova Scotia backwoods using cattle molasses as a base. Burnt sugar or caramel was used to color the smuggled liquor, and oil of rye or bourbon gave it flavor. For the customers who liked their whiskey with a little more bite, bootleggers added iodine to the mixture. For the more die-hard drinkers the moonshiners added an extra generous amount—about two ounces of iodine per quart. Their customers never complained.

"Man, that's good booze," one Chicago customer was heard to say. "Wicked stuff. Burns like fire down my throat."

If iodine was in short supply, the local undertaker would supply embalming fluid to give the hooch an even greater kick. Unfortunately, sometimes the homegrown firewater could be deadly. Some of the less reputable moonshiners who were in a hurry to make another batch seldom cleaned the tubs and copper tubing, and the foul stench could be detected for miles. There are even reports that when the RCMP busted some of these illegal stills, they would find chunks of bone, rat and cat carcasses and insects floating in the mash.

Busted! Prohibition agents dismantle a moonshine still they've raided in a backwoods hideaway.

The rum-running trade that came to life in the Atlantic Provinces during Prohibition provided employment for thousands of Canadians. Many of the young war heroes who came home to the Maritimes from the trenches of Europe after World War I were looking for excitement and a quick dollar. These men provided the manpower on the dozens of smuggling ships carrying load after load of booze to the thirsty Americans. Life was tough in those days. The Canadian economy was struggling to rebound after the war. Money was tight, and work was hard to find. It was a time when some men reluctantly left their maritime homes and took long cross-country treks out west searching for work. Others shunned leaving their families to work for pennies a day on the farms and factories across Canada, and instead manned the ships and trucks that smuggled the booze bound for the United States out of Rum Row.

Many of Atlantic Canada's best and most adventurous fishing captains and crews took to the rum-running trade, and some of them lost their lives in the pursuit. These fearless sailors quickly refitted their schooners for one purpose—to transport illegal liquor while outrunning the law. They installed modified 12-cylinder high horsepower engines, smoke-screen machines and hidden compartments to hide the booze from the searching eyes of customs agents.

The U.S. and Canadian Coast Guards went to work as well, building an armada of swift cutters to intercept the rumrunners. Most were also armed to the teeth with machine guns and one-pound cannon. But tracking down and nabbing the smugglers was an extremely frustrating task for the Coast Guard on both sides of the border. There were dozens if not hundreds of boats operating along legendary Rum Row. If the rumrunners couldn't outrun the Coast Guard, the wily captains could always hide out in one of the thousands of coves or islands along the coast.

When the large "mother ships" slipped past the authorities and successfully arrived at the pre-arranged drop-off zone, its shipment of booze from Canada would be unloaded onto small boats a few miles offshore. Nobody in authority could challenge the ships outside the 12-mile limit of Nova Scotia (later changed to three miles). These small craft, often fishing boats with "souped-up" engines, then surreptitiously transported the booze to shore, where it would go to serve the residences and speakeasies of the northeast from Boston to

Coast Guard patrol boats used to track down smugglers along Rum Row. Two hundred 75-foot boats were built to enforce Prohibition between 1924 and 1925.

~oOo~

New York. Some smugglers burned tires to create a thick black smoke to cover their escape route, and others would douse their running lights, cut engines and drift away under cover of the night and fog.

One of the most thrilling stories from this era is about the Nova Scotia schooner *William S. Macdonald*. In October 1923, Captain Morris Randall of LaHave, Nova Scotia, skippered that three-masted schooner. Randall was a fearless, hard-drinking, swarthy-cheeked Nova Scotian whose life had been spent on the sea. One fall night, he was at home enjoying a rare weekend with his wife and children in LaHave, when two men in gray suits came to his door.

"Mr. Randall, we've been sent by the owners of the *William S. Macdonald*."

Randall knew the ship well. He'd watched it being built in the Lunenburg shipyards five years earlier.

"They'd like to hire you on as captain to pick up a load of rum in Havana and then take it to New Jersey.

"Boys, you tell your people they've come to the right man. If the price is right, they've got themselves a captain!" Randall exclaimed, shaking the men's hands in a powerful grip. "C'mon in, and let's hammer out the details."

They offered Morris Randall $500 a month plus a bonus on delivery. He'd been out of work for a month, so the offer was welcome. Early the next morning, he began selecting his crew. He chose four young teenage boys who were courageous and hard workers. He also hired two old friends who were seasoned seamen. The crew spent the rest of the week setting the canvas and getting the *Macdonald* loaded with provisions and ready for the long voyage. They sailed out of LaHave on October 13, 1923, heading for Cuba. It was a crisp fall morning complete with a clear, blue sky.

The weather was fair all the way to Cuba. The crew spent days on deck and evenings playing cards and gambling. It was Randall's first trip to Cuba, and he was amazed at the similarity to Spain, which he'd seen during the war—beautiful, old buildings, stone arches and old churches.

Randall was working to a tight deadline, but he still allowed his crew one night out on the town to explore Havana nightlife and enjoy the company of the exotic Cuban women. The next day the men were back at work, loading up case after case of dark Cuban rum.

In the morning, they set sail for a place called Sandy Hook, New Jersey, where they would be met by a gangster ship, the *Margaret Bachman*. The trip back to North America was a breeze for the *Macdonald* and crew—fair weather and strong winds carried them northeast to the New Jersey coastline in record time. Randall's instructions were to sail to a point 12 miles off Sandy Hook, wait for the Bachman to arrive and then transfer his $80,000 liquid cargo.

They waited a day and a half for the *Bachman* to arrive. When it did, the two ships pulled up along side each other.

"Ahoy there," Captain Randall yelled. "Let's get to work."

No Coast Guard cutters were in sight, so at 7:00 PM the two crews began transferring the liquor from the *Macdonald* to the *Bachman*. They were almost half finished when the sky grew dark, and it began to rain lightly.

"Sweet Jesus," cursed one of the American deckhands. "Feel that temperature drop."

Suddenly, all hell broke loose. The sky opened up, and a fierce wind began to blow

"Batten down the hatches, boys," Captain Randall yelled.

Randall didn't want to risk the growing storm and the high seas. He now had a nearly empty hold and no ballast to hold the ship stable in the water. The sailors on the *Macdonald* lashed down the sails as the furious gale blew the two schooners apart.

The captain of the *Bachman* immediately ordered his men to hoist the sails and make a run for it. Through pounding 20-foot waves, he sailed out from under the storm and made it safely to Sandy Hook harbor. It was a different story for the *Macdonald*. Within 20 minutes, part of the *Macdonald*'s rigging was torn away, and the ship floundered in the heavy seas. She began taking on water.

Randall's stomach was in knots. In these northern waters, he knew there could be any number of snags, sandbars or rock outcroppings that could be the doom of both his ship and his crew. He wasn't even sure of their exact location. At a loss about the best way to handle the situation, he just stood there thinking.

Finally, Randall decided that it would be foolish to go on.

"Men, we're going to have to beach her or we're going to sink," he screamed into the Atlantic gale.

The men agreed, and they fired up the diesel engines in an attempt to get her to shore before being blown out to sea. But it was too late. The *Macdonald* ran up on the shoals. The heavy seas pounded her against the rocks, threatening to crush the ship. Randall knew all hope was lost.

Although he was as shaken as his crew, he refused to show any signs of fear. He walked out onto the rolling deck in the pelting rain. Doing his best to remain upright, he stood there unprotected from the elements with his hands clasped behind his back. In all his years on the sea, this was the worst storm he'd ever sailed in.

A nearby bolt of lightning quickly brought him back to the present. He fell to his knees and raised his hands and face towards the sky. He prayed out loud as the crew hung on to anything they could to stay on the rolling deck.

"Lord, as the disciples in that boat of long ago, we are at peril upon the storm-tossed sea," Randall prayed. "Please have mercy on us."

Suddenly, the wind died down, and the *Macdonald* broke free of the shoals. In the gray, rain-swept dawn, the *Macdonald* was drifting in the Atlantic, its sails torn away and engines flooded with seawater. The crew raised a distress signal, and the cook put on a pot of coffee. Amazed that they survived the stormy night, the seamen felt their spirits rise.

A few hours later, the funnels of a rescue ship, the *San Manuel*, appeared. The *San Manuel* signaled that she would aid them, and Randall and his crew prepared to abandon ship.

But before they left the *Macdonald*, one of the crew members dropped a torch into the hold, igniting the remaining bootleg liquor. As Randall and his crew reached the deck of the *San Manuel*, he watched with a tear in his eye as the blue flames destroyed his ship. With a sizzle and a hiss, the *William S. Macdonald* slipped into the ocean depths, gone forever.

In the weeks and months to come, Randall never hesitated to tell his incredible story to U.S. and Canadian customs officials. He told the truth and maintained that he had not violated any U.S. liquor laws.

Randall's ship wasn't the only one affected by the fierce Atlantic gale. Several Trans-Atlantic steamers, buffeted and damaged by rough seas, reported being delayed many hours in reaching port. Hundreds of small craft lying in harbors and coves along the coast were also destroyed or swept out to sea.

Another rum-running sea captain who braved the fierce Atlantic weather and the Coast Guard to smuggle booze was Captain Bill McCoy. He earned a reputation as a clever smuggler and sailor who always seemed to be able to stay one step ahead of the authorities. He was a well-respected seaman and fishing boat builder in Nova Scotia who decided that the money was worth the risk and got into the smuggling business during the early years of Prohibition. He bought a schooner named the *Arethusa*; he turned it into a floating liquor store and gave out free samples of various blends of whiskey on board.

McCoy knew a quality boat when he saw it, and the *Arethusa* was well-known for her fine craftsmanship, even though she had a checkered past that would make most superstitious sailors steer clear of the schooner. In 1914, an 18-year-old boy named Louis Amiro was swept off her decks in a fierce storm in the Bay of Fundy. Louis drowned, and his body was never recovered. But Bill McCoy didn't let that bit of morbid history stop him from buying the *Arethusa*.

Destroying the evidence. When threatened with apprehension, rumrunners often set fire to their boats to destroy their illegal cargo rather than risk getting caught with bootleg booze.

To ward off any evil spirits he renamed her the *Tomoka* and registered her as British.

She was a Glouster-type fishing schooner that turned heads in every port. Framed with white oak and held together with 2000 black nails and bronze fasteners, she was planked with oak below and mahogany above the waterline. She also had white pine bulwarks and white oak rail caps. The masts, spars, gaffs and booms were all made from white spruce.

While many suppliers offered watered-down liquor, McCoy got a reputation for selling high-quality stuff at fair prices. He quickly became known as the "founder" of Rum Row. Buyers sought out the *Tomoka* to get "the real McCoy," giving birth to that common expression.

Bill McCoy was a complicated character. He'd never been involved in any illegal activity, and he bought and sold liquor although he was not a drinker himself. Like other rum-running ships' captains, McCoy was intelligent enough to figure out a clever way to avoid the U.S. lawmen. He'd simply hove to outside the magic 12-mile territorial limit to remain immune from prosecution. He then waited for the penny-pinching American gangsters to come to him to strike a deal.

But it was a clever invention of his own design that gained him favor with notorious mobster Al Capone. He met the infamous mob boss in St. Pierre when Capone was staying at the town's hotel and working on a deal with another sea captain regarding a liquor shipment to Boston that was worth more than half a million dollars.

McCoy saw him standing on the dock deep in conversation with a group of men. He could hear the gangster negotiating a deal with the dockhands to unload liquor for 25 cents per case. That worked out to about $20 for a night's work, which was about double what an honest worker could make on St. Pierre and Miquelon.

When the deal was done and the men parted company, McCoy approached the stocky gangster and extended his hand.

"Welcome to St. Pierre, Mr. Capone," McCoy said. "Nice to meet you."

McCoy went on to tell Capone that he was a rumrunner and had made many trips to New York for Capone's colleague, Lucky Luciano.

"I've heard terrible things about him, but he's always treated me right."

Capone smiled. "Do you break as many damn bottles as these guys?" he asked, jerking a thumb over his shoulder at the sailors who were just walking away.

"Funny you should mention that, sir," McCoy said, seizing the opportunity. "I'm rather proud of an invention of mine, and I think you should know about it."

McCoy led Capone up the gangplank of the Tomoka and took him down into the schooner's hold. He could tell Capone was impressed with the well-built ship by the way he slowed down and ran his hands along the rails and mahogany planks.

"She's a beauty, ain't she, sir?"

Capone nodded in agreement.

McCoy took Capone to the far end of the hold where his boys were loading burlap bags. Capone seemed to be puzzled at first.

McCoy explained that he was getting frustrated with all the money he was losing from the glass bottles getting smashed as they were loaded into his ship, so he designed what he called a "burlock." It was a package of six bottles, padded with straw, arranged in a pyramid formation and tightly sewn into burlap bags. Not only did they take up less space than wooden crates and barrels, but the bags could also be tossed around without breaking the glass.

When he ripped open one of the burlocks to show Capone exactly what he was talking about, the mob boss' eyes lit up and he slapped McCoy on the back.

"That's brilliant, Bill," Capone said, with a chuckle. "Welcome to my team!"

Capone also liked the burlocks because, if they had to be thrown overboard during a raid, they sank quickly to the bottom of the sea unlike the wooden crates that bobbed about in the water for weeks. The sacks soon became known as "hams" to the Coast Guard.

Although he never saw Al Capone again, Captain Bill McCoy worked almost exclusively for the Chicago gangster for the next five years. Eventually, McCoy had three boats operating out of Rum Row.

Bringing in rum from Nassau and whiskey from Canada, he made considerable profit. The *Tomoka*, with Captain Bill McCoy at the helm, was one of the best sellers in the rum fleet. It's believed that he sold between 14,000 and 20,000 gallons of liquor over five years.

But in 1929, one late-night incident near the Lunenburg docks scared Bill so much that he decided it was time to change careers. He was out for his nightly stroll and smoking a cigarette. Walking around a stack of lumber, he suddenly came face to face with a man who pointed a .45-caliber revolver at his face.

"I got a warning for you, McCoy," the gunman said. "Like it or not, we're hijacking your ship and the hooch tonight, and I don't want no bloodshed. If you know what's good for you, walk away or we'll kill ya."

It didn't take Captain McCoy long to make a decision.

"She's all yours, boyo."

He slowly turned around and then headed quickly for home, his shoulders tense, half expecting a bullet in the back.

It was the last straw for Captain Bill McCoy. He'd had one too many chance encounters at sea with both pirates and well-armed Coast Guard officials. McCoy, like other rumrunners, generally traveled unarmed, relying on the speed of his boats, his navigational abilities and smoke screens to elude pursuers. But gunfire was becoming a common sound along Rum Row. McCoy wanted no part of the bloodshed that was beginning to stain the Atlantic Ocean and the shores of Nova Scotia. He decided to call it quits and retired.

As pirates began attacking rumrunners, more and more booze was being dumped overboard or hidden in the swamps and woods of the Maritime islands. It was a common occurrence for residents to find liquor that had been dumped, so the locals who salvaged the liquor got involved in smuggling.

One story tells of a young boy who lived near Chester Basin, Nova Scotia. He was out walking one evening along the beach when he noticed a piece of paper between two rocks. He bent down to pick it up, and to his surprise, it was attached to a long piece of string. He followed the string that was buried in a few inches of sand to the base of an old maple tree, where it suddenly disappeared into the earth. He dug until a huge hole opened up. In it, he found a rumrunner's stash. The string was looped through the handles of eight one-gallon ceramic jugs filled with Cuban cane rum. He covered up the hole with branches and ran to tell his grandfather (whom he knew liked his toddy of rum). The grandfather came back with the boy, and together they hauled out all the jugs. They then tied the string to the horns of an old, bleached cattle skull they had found, refilled the hole and covered up the string along the beach. They chuckled as they walked back to the farm, carefully pushing the clanking jugs along in a rusty wheelbarrow. They were imagining the surprised looks on the faces of the rumrunners when they returned for their stash. When they got back to the farm, the two hid the jugs beneath the floorboards of the grandfather's barn.

A lot of booze was brought into the Bay of Fundy during Prohibition and stashed by rumrunners with the Coast Guard in hot pursuit. One day in 1928, two sisters were playing not far from a beach near Windsor, Ontario. Despite their father's warning, the girls were playing near some piles of old logs when they discovered some sod covering a hole. They pulled back the sod to find several kegs labeled Black Diamond Rum stacked end to end deep down inside. They went home and told their mother.

"Don't say a word to anyone," their mother said. "The men who put that rum there will be very angry."

But a local bootlegger got wind of the girl's find, and the next evening he went with some friends down to the beach. They soon discovered more liquor in many different stashes and loaded up more than 50 kegs, which they hauled back to a shed on the outskirts of town. True to eastern hospitality, the bootleggers offered up some of the kegs of rum as free liquid refreshment at Windsor's town hall dances that winter. People came from miles around to pass around the bootleg booze and sing and dance to Maritime tunes until the sun came up.

As competition increased among the rumrunners, so did the power of their boats. One rumrunner, based out of Southport, Prince Edward Island, built a boat called the *Good Luck*. The 65-foot Jonesport boat was powered by twin 300-hp Sterlings with twin rudders and a silencer the size of a 55-gallon drum. If the weather was right, the *Good Luck* could make the run from Truro, Nova Scotia, to Bar Harbor, Maine, in 18 hours. So, in response to the new and more powerful boats being used by the rumrunners, the Coast Guard was forced to become even more aggressive.

The man in charge of the Coast Guard at the time was U.S. Commandant William E. Reynolds. He was frustrated with the lack of resources to combat the rapidly growing smuggling industry.

The 65-year-old was regarded as intelligent and tough with a long and well-respected naval career. He joined the Revenue Cutter service when he was 18 and quickly climbed through the ranks. He'd fought in several fierce naval battles during the Spanish-American War and was appointed Chief of Staff, 12th Naval District during World War I.

Reynolds was aware that if he didn't expand his small and aging fleet quickly, his mission to stop the smugglers would fail. In addition, the media had picked up on the story, and

it was now public knowledge that the Coast Guard was struggling in the battle to stop booze smuggling. Reynolds, a proud
man, took the criticism personally.

In October 1923, he put in an urgent request to the U.S.
government for help. In his proposal, Reynolds stressed that
he needed at least $20 million to expand and upgrade his
fleet. To fight the smugglers, he requested 200 more cruisers,
90 speedboats and a budget to hire and train more crew. The
government immediately gave Reynolds the green light.

The most famous Coast Guard vessels that Reynolds added
became known as six-bitters. These stripped-down, souped-
up patrol boats were not built for comfort but for speed. Fast
and tough, these powerful boats could zip in and out of harbors at speeds up to 30 knots. They became one of the Coast
Guard's most valuable tools in its crime-fighting arsenal.

Reynolds also added several World War I destroyers to his
growing fleet. Many of these 1000-ton warhorses were in poor
shape and needed major engine and structural repairs. The
lumbering four-stackers were also underpowered. Reynolds
ordered complete engine overhauls and the ships stripped
down and repaired. When the renovations were complete,
some of the destroyers could reach speeds of over 30 knots.
With 3500 new crewmembers hired, trained and ready to staff
his new fighting force, Reynolds was well prepared for battle.
The U.S. Coast Guard launched its revamped and deadly flotilla
in the war against the rum smugglers between 1924 and 1926.

The battle against smuggling turned into a long and
bloody campaign at sea and on land. It wasn't just the sailors,
lawmen and outlaws who fell victim to fierce smuggling skir-
mishes. Civilians also got caught in the crossfire. It's estimated
that some 200 innocent people were killed in shootouts
between warring gangsters. That works out to about 20 per-
cent per year who died in the bloody Prohibition violence
from 1920 to 1933.

One story tells of a rum-running ship's deck stained with blood. The *Black Duck* was a fast 50-footer equipped with airplane engines and a smoke-screen machine that left a thick, oily, black smoke in its wake. In 1929, the *Duck* and her crew were caught in the wrong place at the wrong time.

The Coast Guard ship *CG-290*, piloted by Alexander C. Cornell was patrolling the frigid waters off Jamestown, Rhode Island in December 1929 when the rumrunner the *Black Duck* suddenly appeared out of the fog. The *Duck* was moving exceptionally fast. Cornell estimated her speed at about 30 knots. She was running with no lights, and that made him suspicious. When he realized the rumrunner was on a direct collision course with his cutter, Cornell set off the warning siren and ordered the powerful searchlight turned on. There was no response and The *Duck* kept rumbling towards him.

She was only 75 feet away when Cornell shouted, "Open fire. Now."

The machine gunner pulled the trigger and sprayed a quick burst into the air above the *Duck*. Suddenly, she veered away and turned to run. This time, Cornell gave the order for the gunner to fire directly at the fleeing ship. But Cornell knew it was pointless to try to pursue the *Duck*. The cutter's speed was no match for the high-powered rumrunner. Frustrated, he resumed his course. Then, about 45 minutes later, the *Black Duck* suddenly reappeared alongside the cutter. Startled, Cornell ran to the deck.

"We've got wounded here. Please help," cried someone from the *Duck*.

Cornell drew his revolver and ordered the cutter be brought alongside the *Duck*. On deck, two sailors were dead and two others seriously wounded with bullet wounds from the Coast Guard's machine gun. The wounded men were carried onto the cutter and the *Duck* was towed to Jamestown.

Five hundred cases of liquor were found piled on the deck of the rumrunner, and the *Black Duck* was confiscated. The Coast Guard mechanics marveled at the boat's high speed because of her modified high performance diesel engines. The U.S. Navy eventually transformed the rumrunner into *CG-808* and used her speed to bring down other smuggling ships with great success.

But it was a short-wave radio set that shut down many Canadian rumrunners off the eastern seaboard in 1926. Fourteen-year-old Fletcher Henderson was sitting in his bedroom in Bucksport, Maine, one fall night, listening to his homemade short-wave radio. He was a member of the Bar Harbor Amateur Radio Club, and when his homework was done, he often spent evenings listening to broadcasts from all over the world.

In the 1920s a short-wave radio, wave meter and code books were state of the art technology, similar to the internet and cell phones today. Radios allowed rumrunners to stay in touch with a home base on shore. A land operator could alert the crew of a pirate ship loaded with booze if the federal lawmen were about to conduct a raid. Rumrunners often stole the Coast Guard's secret code so they could monitor their radio frequency and track their whereabouts.

On this particular night, Fletcher was spinning through the frequencies below the broadcast bands when he picked up a signal that didn't sound familiar.

"Eagle One to Eagle two. Where are you? Over," crackled the gruff voice on the radio.

"The Eagle lands at dawn," Fletcher heard. He was startled by how crisp and clear the response came through his radio's tiny speaker.

Fletcher called his father into his bedroom and told him what he'd heard. At first, his dad thought it was kids playing a game, but when he heard reference to unloading cargo into horse-drawn wagons down on the shore near Bucksport, he decided it was best to report the strange signals to the local police.

The police alerted the FBI, and they immediately launched an investigation into the mysterious radio messages. For weeks, government agents listened to the signals. Their investigation revealed that gangsters were using an amazingly clever yet simple code. Its main secret was the use of a series of seemingly unconnected words strung randomly together. "Instrumental stone cold juice incorporated," for example, would be broadcast over and over.

The agents also discovered that the call letters the gangsters were using did not correspond to any known amateur's station lawfully operating at the time. Once the agents figured out the frequency on which the pirate signals were being broadcast, they soon solved the case. One night, the agents tuned in and listened as the smugglers struggled for three hours to contact their cohorts on land to arrange a drop-off. When the frustrated ship's captain finally made contact with his land base, he was in such a hurry to get the job done that he ignored the code and spelled out the gang's plans in detail.

The surprised agents couldn't believe their good luck.

"Dear mother of God," the government agent whispered, "those crazy Canucks are unloading their booze 20 miles down the shore!"

They quickly radioed the Coast Guard with the position of the operation. On March 30, 1927, at about 11:30 PM, U.S. federal lawmen moved in and nabbed the smugglers and the gangsters in the middle of unloading a shipment of Canadian whiskey smuggled in from the St. Lawrence Seaway.

Along with the smugglers and mob contacts, the rumrunner's land-based wireless operator was also arrested. And the timing for the arrest could not have been more perfect.

Four local men in two small skiffs had transferred the entire shipment from a mother ship to shore. They had then loaded 120 kegs of rum onto four wagons, 30 kegs to a wagon, each drawn by a single black horse. It was one of the biggest bootleg busts in Maine's history. Each wagon carried over a ton of illegal hooch!

Malcolm MacMasters was running the land-based wireless operation out of his house on a hill overlooking the Atlantic Ocean. He was held on $30,000 bail, not only for violation of the Volstead Act, but also for transmission without either a station or operator's license. It was the first time the Radio Act penalties were applied to such an offender.

With the discovery of the main transmitter of the rum ring, the Prohibition forces crippled the communication system built up at great cost by the bootleggers. But apparently another secret installation flashed a message warning the seagoing boats filled with liquor to turn back because of the raid. That radio was never found.

From then on, it was easy for the government wireless operators to nab the smugglers' ships. In all, 23 smugglers' ships, sailing from St. Pierre to Bermuda, with stops from Boston to Atlantic City, and a swarm of American gangster speedboats were stopped and their crews arrested.

The U.S. Coast Guard was amazed at the complexity of the radio network used by Canadian mother ships and the gangster's wireless home base on land. It is thought that all the ships, including the speedboats, were equipped with radios and were directed by the main station located in the house captured on the Highland hilltop.

Smaller operators were gradually forced out of the business, replaced by faster, larger boats. One of the new breed of inshore boats that did well in the business was the *Maybe*. Built at Southwest Harbor, Maine, she was a typical 50'–80' boat built for the trade between 1927 and 1935.

The *Maybe* had a 1500 gallon fuel tank located below the ship's engine and out of the range of bullets. Capable of 33 knots, she was a round bottom, flush sheer boat with a 16-foot beam and 4 1/2-foot draft. Captained by a man from Pembroke, Maine, the *Maybe* had a successful life as a rumrunner, but like all rumrunners was subject to threats presented by the Coast Guard and pirates. One late December night, while being pursued by the Coast Guard, the *Maybe* dumped a large load of liquor overboard in shallow water at Misham Point, South Dartmouth, Massachusetts. It was discovered by a boy fishing for sea bass with his grandfather off the shore and quickly and quietly loaded up and taken home.

It's a good thing the mobsters didn't come along at the same time the boy and his grandfather were picking up those kegs of booze. Gangs whose hooch was hijacked took a dim view of those who would steal from them. In 1931, Thomas Farrell Jr. and Jacob Antilety, both 21, were walking in Southampton, Maine, when they were kidnapped by mobsters who accused them of stealing booze that had been dumped overboard during a storm two days before. They were taken to a farmhouse outside Southampton, handcuffed to a radiator in the kitchen, and in the dim light of the refrigerator were tortured all night with a heated potato masher applied to their feet. The color drained from the men's faces under the intense torture, and they passed out from the searing pain. The gangsters slapped them awake and then dragged them outside where they were put in a car, driven to a remote road and abandoned in a ditch. Just as dawn was breaking, a milkman driving a horse-drawn wagon found them slumped over and leaning against a signpost. He picked them up, put them in the back of his wagon and took them to hospital for treatment. Even before the victims were released, everyone in town was talking about the vicious attack. The message was clear— the mobsters, despite their expensive clothes, fancy cars and celebrity status, were nothing more than brutal thugs who would stop at nothing to protect their cargo.

However, the underworld's violent liquor-smuggling rackets soon came to an end. By the early, '30s, American politicians and the public could see that "The Noble Experiment" had been a dismal failure. Instead of improving people's health and their quality of life, it had ushered in one of the bloodiest and most crime-ridden eras in U.S. history. Prohibition fueled the rise of the powerful Mafia syndicates, spawning a ruthless, greedy monster with tentacles creeping into all aspects of society, from labor unions to the justice and political arenas. By 1932, the backlash was enormous. Prohibition had become unpopular with the American public. The Democrats used the abolition of Prohibition as a campaign issue, and their candidate, Franklin D. Roosevelt, was swept into the White House.

On March 13, 1933, a few days after he was sworn in as president, Roosevelt called a special session of the Congress to revise the Volstead Act to legalize the sale of alcohol to provide needed tax revenue. His request was granted, and national alcohol prohibition law was repealed effective immediately. Overnight, Prohibition ended in the United States. America was no longer dry.

A popular country song of the day sums up the mood of the American people:

> *Roosevelt was elected,*
> *Elected in time*
> *Went to the treasury and found one dime*
> *Got back liquor*
> *And got back beer,*
> *Heap better times in the next four years.*
>
> –Anonymous, traditional folk song

When "The Noble Experiment" ended in the United States in 1933, the curtain also came down on one of the most exciting eras in Canadian history. The "Golden Years" of the rumrunners along Rum Row was over.

It's difficult, if not impossible, to grasp the enormous fiscal impact Prohibition had on the economy of the Maritimes. Accounting records and ship logbooks cannot be considered even remotely accurate, but it is safe to say that thousands of gallons of good Canadian whiskey flowed across the border during this time, and hundreds of families in the Atlantic Provinces prospered as a result.

Even today, a few enterprising Maritimers continue to make a few extra bucks selling bootleg booze or moonshine on the black market. If a house party is running into the wee hours, the liquid refreshments are getting low and the guests aren't ready to call it a night, everyone knows the local bootlegger who will sell them a bottle or two of liquor or a case of beer.

And deep in the backwoods of the Atlantic Provinces, moonshiners continue to cook up their favorite batches of home brew using secret recipes passed down through the generations. To this day, if you know the right people and promise to keep your mouth shut, you can still buy a bottle of high-test hooch cooked up by the old-timers in their trusty old copper stills. You know it's good booze when you light a spoonful and the flame burns a brilliant blue. It's affectionately known by the locals as River Rum, and it's some of the finest white lightning around. But don't breathe a word, my dear reader. You didn't hear it here.

CHAPTER SIX

The *I'm Alone* (1923–1929)

Remember, yes, I remember well
The most famous rumrunner of them all
She was the schooner from Lunenburg, *I'm Alone*
And in the Gulf of Mexico she went down
Under fire from a Yankee cutter
On the high seas, outside treaty water.
Oh, *I'm Alone*
A long way from Lunenburg she went down
Because skipper John Randell wouldn't heave-to
On the *I'm Alone*.

–From the folk song *The Sinking of the I'm Alone* by Wade Hemsworth

DEEP IN THE HEART OF WHAT WAS ONCE RUM ROW, on the southeast shore of Nova Scotia, is one of the most famous shipbuilding communities in the world. Lunenburg was established in 1753 and became the birthplace of many well-known ships including Canada's most famous sailing vessel, the Bluenose, built in 1921. But one of the most infamous ships ever built in the Lunenburg shipyards was the *I'm Alone*. She ran rum from Canada to the United States for five years before being sunk by Prohibition agents in a fierce gun battle on the high seas in the Gulf of Mexico. Her incredible story became fodder for folklore and legend. In fact, the entire tale was immortalized in the old sea shanty, The Sinking of the *I'm Alone* by Wade Hemsworth.

In September 1923, hundreds of people from miles around crowded into the Lunenburg shipyards to watch the launch of the latest schooner to be built in the port community. The *I'm Alone* was one of five ships built in Lunenburg that year. Shipbuilding was the livelihood for most of the people in the area, and when a new ship was ready to be launched, it was a celebration. The event overflowed with pomp and ceremony. The red and white pennants that adorned the handsome two-masted schooner's rigging for the occasion flapped in the September breeze. The owners of Smith & Rhuland Limited, the company that built the ship, were seated under a white tent with other shipping officials and town dignitaries. The mayor waved his hand for the ceremony to begin. The brass band stopped playing in mid-song, and the crowd leaned forward, straining to hear the priest's words as he blessed the ship. When he was done, the shipyard's brass bell tolled once, and seven men cut the ropes holding the ship on the building platform. With a creaking groan, the handsome schooner slowly slid backwards down the ramp and splashed stern first into the Atlantic Ocean. A mighty cheer went up from the crowd. A successful launch was always great news for everyone.

It was a Boston gangster who built the $18,000, two-masted ship in Lunenburg in 1923 for one purpose: to smuggle whiskey from Canada to the U.S. The reason the Boston mobster had her built in Canada was so that the ship would not be subject to American Prohibition laws.

In 1928, the *I'm Alone* was sold and placed under the command of Captain John Randell. Forty-nine-year-old John Randell was grizzled and aged beyond his years with a commanding baritone voice. He had grayish-brown hair, a weathered face and deep lines around his eyes from squinting into the ocean horizon. Randell was hired by his Boston boss only two months earlier for $500 a month.

He was born on January 1, 1879, in Ship Cove, Trinity Bight, Newfoundland (present-day Port Rexton) and grew up on the sea. He came from a long line of sailors with a documented history going back 500 years to Bridport in Dorsetshire, England. His great-great grandfather, Captain John Randell, sailed to the New World in 1715 when the British took Newfoundland from France.

Captain Randell's exploits as a war hero were well known. He gave up the sea for a horse briefly when he joined the Royal Artillery in the Boer War, and he was decorated for bravery on the battlefield. When the war was over, he enjoyed some success as an amateur prizefighter. During World War I, he became a British Naval Officer and spent most of the war hunting down and destroying German submarines off the English Coast. King George V personally decorated him with the Distinguished Service Cross for his bravery in battle.

He was strong, quick with his fists and walked with a swagger, but he was also known for his fondness for well-tailored and expensive clothes. He always took a dinner jacket and dress shirts on all his voyages. But his time in the war left him with a hunger for excitement and adventure. When he was offered the job to command the rumrunner *I'm Alone* on his return to civilian life, he couldn't resist.

Randell had also lost money and a ship in a recent business venture, making the offer even more attractive than a long, cold winter in Nova Scotia working on a fishing boat. It seemed a good way to return to another line of sailing once his bank account had been filled. So, he took the offer and began hiring his crew.

One of the first sailors to sign up was 19-year-old James Barrett. James was a tall, handsome, lanky lad with muscular arms and big, callused hands from working on his grandfather's farm. He had jet black, wavy hair and striking blue eyes.

Barrett was born in a two-story house on the Glooscap Trail in 1909 in Summerville, Nova Scotia, a small seafaring settlement on the west side of Minas Basin. In the summer of 1928, Captain John Thomas Randell hired the young, wide-eyed sailor for $75 a month to work aboard the schooner *I'm Alone*.

On October 2, 1928, Barrett showed up, nervous but eager for adventure at the Lunenburg dock with his duffel bag, joining the seven other crewmen Randell had hired.

"James Barrett reporting for duty, sir!" Barrett said in a shaky voice. Barrett liked Captain Randell from the moment he shook the man's strong hand.

The Captain smiled. "C'mon along, son. I'll introduce you to your crewmates."

It was a good team of able-bodied seamen—some seasoned veterans and others, like James, a little green under the collar. But they made up for their inexperience with enthusiasm for an exciting life on the sea. Two other sailors hired were Edward Bouchard and Eddie Young. There was also assistant engineer Jens Jensen, mate John George Williams and engineer Chester Hobbs. A fellow named William Wordsworth was the cook, and Leon Mainguy was the ship's boatswain.

Captain Randell gave his new crew a tour of the magnificent two-masted schooner. She was not only equipped with sails but she also had two 100-hp semi-diesel oil-burning engines to help her speed along. The men marveled at the workmanship. She was a luxurious beauty and admired for miles around. The *I'm Alone* was 125 feet long and 27 feet wide at the broadest point.

Of course, sailing was not an easy way of life. Nothing comes easy on the ocean. The days were long, and the backbreaking work was nonstop. The crew spent a week loading provisions and getting the ship ready for its dangerous mission. They spent a good portion of their days polishing,

The ship and crew of the Nova Scotia rumrunner *I'm Alone* in happier times. Captain John Randell (center, dressed in a suit) with crew around him. Edward Bouchard (sailor), Jens Jensen (assistant engineer), John George Williams (mate), Chester Hobbs (engineer), James Barrett (sailor), William Wordsworth (cook), Eddie Young (sailor).

The *I'm Alone* was sunk by U.S. Coast Guard patrol boats in the Gulf of Mexico in March 1929. One of the crew, Leon Mainguy, drowned in the incident. The Canadian government sued the United States, and the ensuing legal battle garnered worldwide attention.

cleaning and making everything shipshape for the voyage. James was excited about the prospect of finally setting sail, but his stomach flip-flopped at the thought of the adventures that lay ahead.

Before the captain gave the order to hoist anchor, he called the crew on deck.

"Gather 'round boys. There's something I have to do before we leave."

He reached into the breast pocket of his pea coat and pulled out a shiny silver dollar.

"Before we head out to sea, I always like to make a little down payment to the ocean," the captain said, "for good luck, good winds and a safe voyage."

James watched the captain's face closely to see if he was joking, but the captain's eyes were closed and his craggy jaw set as he flipped the coin high into the air and over the side. The crew watched the silver coin disappear into the murky depths of the harbor.

"Anchors away!" The captain broke the silence. "Let's be off then, boys."

The anchor was a 200-pound hook attached to 100 feet of heavy chain and raised by a double-handled hand crank. James watched in amazement as two of the strongest sailors put their backs to the task. Bouchard and Long took hold of the big hand crank on deck, and they grunted and strained until the anchor was above the water. It took them at least 25 minutes to hoist up the anchor.

Captain Randell then gave the order to fire up the engines, and soon the schooner was chugging out of the Lunenburg harbor heading to Rum Row.

The knots in James' stomach began to disappear as he focused his attention to his tasks on board. The crew worked hard together as a team, raising the heavy canvas sails hand over hand to the top of the mast. The ship surged ahead, and the drone of the engine ceased as the sails filled and took over the work. At sea, far from land, he often stood on the forward deck watching the water rush by the sleek hull and breathing in the salt air mixed with the aromas of wood and canvas. During the evenings, the men sat on deck gazing at the stars, smoking, drinking cups of rum and telling stories. James was nervous and shy; he'd never been to sea before. Some of the crew were seasoned sailors, having made their living as fishermen before they turned to a life of smuggling. Looking around at his fellow shipmates, James realized they all had one thing in common—they took pride in the job they were about to do, despite their illegal mission.

The first stop along Rum Row was St. Pierre, where they picked up their first cargo of liquor to be delivered to Portland, Maine. St. Pierre was one of a group of French-owned islands 16 miles off the southwest coast of Newfoundland. Most of the liquor stored on the island was produced in Québec and Ontario. Canadian distilleries unloaded as many as 300,000 cases of alcohol per week in St. Pierre's main harbor, where boats such as the *I'm Alone* would then haul the precious cargo south of the border. The cargo was almost always five-gallon kegs of rum packed in wooden cases filled with straw. The *I'm Alone* could carry about 2700 cases.

One of the primary sources of the bootleg liquor smuggled out of Rum Row to the United States was Sam Bronfman's distillery in the Montréal suburb of LaSalle, Québec. This whiskey wasn't the potentially fatal wood alcohol blend that was being made south of the border to quench the thirst of the Prohibition-thirsty Americans. Nor was it the "bathtub gin" packaged in tin cans that poisoned and killed thousands of Americans. This Canadian liquor was Sam Bronfman's high-quality whiskey, aged, carefully blended and legally made in Québec and sold to rumrunners. American gangsters couldn't get enough of it. Rumrunners would transport thousands of cases of Bronfman booze out of Québec in trucks and trains to the East Coast and then by boat to the islands of St. Pierre and Miquelon. It was then up to the rum-running ships to smuggle the cargo into American waters, where it would be picked up by mobsters and distributed across America in the speakeasies and blind pigs.

One of the first American gangsters to set up a rum-running racket was the infamous mobster Al Capone. In the '20s and early '30s, the island people were well aware of Capone's operation because many residents were on the gangster's payroll.

Capone even visited the islands in the mid '20s to ensure that his smuggling operation was running smoothly. The stocky gangster was sometimes seen wandering around town wearing a straw hat and chewing on a fat stogie. Just about every basement in St. Pierre and Miquelon was converted into a warehouse for Capone's bootlegged booze.

Al Capone set up his base of operations at the Robert Hotel on St. Pierre. One of the reasons he came to St. Pierre was to try to find a solution to a problem that was costing him thousands of dollars. The wooden whiskey crates filled with glass bottles made a great deal of noise clinking together as they were unloaded at Fire Island, New York. No matter how carefully the sailors unloaded the liquid cargo, the clanking bottles made such a racket that the American Federal Customs agents were alerted. In addition, much of the booze was lost because the bottles broke in the cases as they were being hastily unloaded onto mobster speedboats. After discussing the problem with one of his ships' captains, the seaman came up with a clever way to quiet the operation. Captain Bill McCoy suggested replacing the cumbersome wooden crates with burlap sacks and packing the bottles in straw for safe transport. Capone was delighted with the idea and immediately ordered his dock workers to transfer the booze from crates to sacks. The discarded wooden crates began piling up along the shore.

Oddly enough, the empty wooden crates were a boon to the islanders. There are practically no trees on St. Pierre and Miquelon, and the wood from the more than 350,000 wooden cases and barrels a year that Capone and his boys left behind on the French Islands created a housing boom. To this day, many of the homes built during that period are made out of wood from Sam Bronfman's wooden liquor crates. One in particular is called the "Cutty Sark Villa."

Prohibition was so profitable on the French islands that flags were flown at half-mast when the Volstead Act was repealed in 1933, and truckers, sailors and the townsfolk held a mock funeral. Many otherwise average, law-abiding citizens, such as Captain Randell and his crew, earned big money smuggling booze because they bought it for 80 cents per quart and sold it for $40 per 12-quart case.

Once at sea, the endless number of chores aboard ship made it easy for James and the rest of the crew to forget that they were really outlaws transporting illegal merchandise. For the most part, the *I'm Alone* could easily slip by Coast Guard cutters at night. Captain Randell ran his schooner without lights, and two ships could pass one another within short range without seeing the other. The strict rule on board was that if any of the crew wanted to smoke, they had to go down below to the engine room for fear the glow of the cigarette could be seen by the authorities and give away their position.

But on December 21, 1928, on one of James' voyages to the U.S., he found himself in the middle of a frightening ordeal with the American Coast Guard. Similar to the drug war of today, busting booze smugglers along the U.S. border kept American federal agents busy full time.

The *I'm Alone* was anchored just outside the 12-mile limit off Portland, Maine, when the Coast Guard came upon her and shone its searchlight on the ship. But because the *I'm Alone* was outside the 12-mile limit, the Coast Guard couldn't board her.

The term "12-mile limit" was used as a typical speed and distance figure. The new law complicated matters somewhat and required careful work by Coast Guard navigators to provide sufficient proof that seizures were unarguably within the requisite boundaries. And enforcing the new 12-mile limit was not as simple as it sounded. Technically, it was an "hour's steaming distance," thus a foreign mother ship was liable to seizure if she was in contact with any American boat within an hour's steaming distance from shore. If the contact boat could run at 20 knots, her mother ship could be seized as far as 20 miles out.

But if Captain Randell prided himself on one thing, it was that he always made sure the *I'm Alone* worked outside territorial limits. On this day, he ordered a smoke screen, and the Coast Guard went to the leeward looking for them. The Canadian schooner lost its trackers but was picked up again, so Captain Randell ordered another smoke screen. But the American got the *I'm Alone* in its spotlight and opened fire with a deck-mounted machine gun.

James heard the bullets whistling through the air and slamming into the side of the boat. He thought the tracer bullets looked like fireflies buzzing overhead. He quickly took refuge down below.

He heard the Coast Guard captain yell, "Do that again, and I'll blow you out of the Atlantic Ocean."

It was too late. The wind filled the *I'm Alone*'s sails, and under cover of the oily smoke screen, she quietly slipped away. But gray clouds were building, and it wasn't long before the skies opened up. With a tremendous crash, a fierce thunderstorm surrounded them. Captain Randell ordered the engines started, and they began a zigzagging course that left the Coast Guard cutter far behind.

James sat shivering on the deck. Even with his oilskins on, he was drenched to the skin. Waves broke over the hull, sending hundreds of gallons of icy water washing over his feet. Above him, the rigging creaked and keened. Others like him, who didn't like the idea of being trapped below decks, sat huddled together topside.

He thought of his mother, who would be baking Christmas cookies. He thought of his father, who would be reading the newspaper beside the fire. And he thought of his sister, who would be eagerly anticipating a late night visit from St. Nick. He'd never felt so alone.

After two days at sea, the *I'm Alone* limped back into Halifax harbor on the Nova Scotia coast. As Captain Randell surveyed the damage from the fierce storm and the bullet holes, his heart was full of sorrow and anger. At the dock, he hired local shipbuilders to hoist the boat out of the water and begin repairs on her. Meanwhile, the crew went ashore for some rest and relaxation.

James checked into the local hotel and fell into a deep sleep. The rest of the crew immediately went to the tavern downstairs and quickly settled into a session of rum drinking and poker playing with the locals. As James drifted off, he heard the sounds of the crew's laughter and the faint strains of music from a phonograph.

Back at the ship, Captain Randell was nervous, his usual smile gone. He stood by the rail watching the workers repair his boat, drumming his fingers on the cold metal, impatient to sail away and sell his liquid cargo.

"C'mon boys, time is money. Let's get a move on. If you get me on the sea by tomorrow morning, there's a case of rum in it for each and every one of ya."

He also knew that the sooner he got his men out of Halifax and away from the tavern, the better off he'd be. He didn't want his crew getting into any trouble with the locals.

James got a knock on his door that night and was told to report for duty. When he got to the ship, the crew was hard at work preparing for its next voyage. Supplies were loaded, the decks scrubbed and the sails washed. Once again, the *I'm Alone* was ready to set sail.

It was a bright, frosty winter's day, and a sharp southwest wind was blowing. The skipper, the spare hand and James got the stops off the sails and everything ready for hoisting. At 1:30 in the afternoon, they sailed out of Halifax harbor, heading for Boston.

An American speedboat was scheduled to meet them at the territorial limit off the U.S. shore. They arrived off the coast of Boston to find the seas shrouded in thick fog. After sailing in circles, they finally spotted the American's speedboat in the distance. They had to move quickly to meet the gangster vessel and get their boat unloaded.

They were almost to the U.S. boat when James heard the gansters hollering.

"Hurry up! We just got word that the Coast Guard is on its way here. They will be here in about an hour and a half!"

The crew took their positions so that they could unload as quickly as possible. The men formed a line and began passing the cases of booze along. One of the American sailors muttered that he had a bad feeling about the entire operation. The time flew by as they unloaded.

The next thing James knew, the boatswain shouted, "I see them! Let's go! Let's go!"

They still had nearly one-third of the cargo aboard the ship. Captain Randell yelled, "Pull this boat around, and let's get out of here. Right now!"

The throttle was at maximum, and the *I'm Alone* slowly turned out to sea.

The boatswain hollered to the captain, "Get this boat going and fast! Move it, move it!"

James heart lurched into his throat when he heard the captain say, "It doesn't look good for us."

A police raid nets a massive haul of hundreds of barrels of bootleg booze in a warehouse.

~✖~

Fortunately, the fog was so thick that it was almost impossible for the Coast Guard to track them. The *I'm Alone* just barely had enough time to get deeper into international waters.

The cook fell to his knees, a big smile on his face showing his relief.

"I thought we'd had it," he laughed, nervously. He liked to live dangerously, and he got a big thrill out of the chase.

But James felt as if his chest would explode.

A month later, on a smuggling run to Atlantic City, Captain Randell decided to take a chance and get closer to shore because there was a big harbor, and the captain could get the *I'm Alone* right in up to the dock under cover of darkness. Engine silencers allowed the schooner to glide in undetected. The mobsters brought in furniture vans, unloaded the liquor and moved it to a warehouse in the city.

But custom officials were often just as crooked as the rum smugglers. They'd stop the furniture vans loaded with booze, take half the shipment for themselves, hide it and then call the media to take pictures as they smashed the remaining kegs with axes at the side of the road. While the pictures on the front page of the papers showed the great job government agents were doing to stop the evil rum smugglers, they were actually stocking their own liquor cabinets at home.

Once in the port of Atlantic City, the crew of the *I'm Alone* had what looked like an easy task. The seas in the harbor were calm and as smooth as glass. They began unloading at a dock into the vans and had unloaded half the cargo, about 1000 cases, when all hell broke loose. The night sky became as bright as day as American agents fired off several flares. The captain yelled for everyone to get back aboard. The crew slipped the lines, lit a smoke screen, making them nearly invisible in the foggy night, and they slipped out of the harbor heading south. The last thing they saw were customs agents rounding up the American gangsters into a paddy wagon. Captain Randell slipped out of the harbor, headed up the eastern seaboard and sold the rest of his load (about 1500 cases) on Fire Island, New York.

This time the mob met the *I'm Alone* 12 miles out from shore in seven speedboats equipped with false bottoms. The gangsters pulled up on the starboard side of the schooner, and James and his crew handed crate after crate down to the Americans. The midnight seas were calm, the moon was bright, and James could see a small hatch door going down from one bottom to the next in the gangster's boat. Once a crate was on board the speedboat, two of the goons would slide down the hatch on their stomachs into the dark secret hole where the liquid cargo was stacked tightly end to end until the space was filled.

After the boats were loaded, another boat appeared loaded with fish. The Americans dumped the fish over the false bottom, hiding the hatch cover and giving the appearance that the boat contained nothing but cod. James chuckled because he could tell from the complaints of the gangsters that they weren't too happy with having to finish their trip smelling like fish.

On one trip, the *I'm Alone* was sailing from St. Pierre with a big load when the rudder broke. They had to head into Mahone Bay, Nova Scotia to repair it. They unloaded the cargo and stashed it on shore in an old well because the ship was taking on water.

Once repairs were made, they stopped in Lunenburg. Captain Randell had an idea to increase his profits. They anchored in the harbor, and Randell had James and Eddie row into town every few days to get fresh water. They began cutting the liquor, mixing a gallon and a half of water to every five gallons of rum. The rum was so strong that cutting it didn't make a difference to the smell or color to the liquor-starved Americans. The gangsters never caught on.

Now the *I'm Alone* was anything but alone. Dozens, if not hundreds, of rum-running ships based in Nova Scotia smuggled booze to the U.S. mob on the high seas. But on March 20, 1929, the *I'm Alone* was involved in a violent cat and mouse incident that forever carved its place in history.

The crew had just sailed to the Gulf of Mexico from St. Pierre fully loaded with rum. The *I'm Alone* was anchored off the coast of New Orleans with 2800 cases on board. The weather was fair, and the boat rocked gently in the water, the only sound a faint squeaking of ropes rubbing on wood.

Captain Randell was waiting for word from his underworld connections in the Big Easy to find out when and where his cargo would be picked up. He was getting nervous. Randell was broke, short on supplies after the long trip and he'd been anchored off the coast for two days. To make matters worse, the crew reported that a Coast Guard cutter, the *Wolcott*, had them under surveillance.

At 5:00 AM on March 20, 1929, the *Wolcott* headed directly for the *I'm Alone*. The *Wolcott*'s boatswain Frank Paul recorded the rumrunner's position at nearly 11 miles from shore. He signaled Randell to stop.

Captain Randell ordered his crew to move the ship seaward, but before they could make any headway, the captain of the *Wolcott* shouted out, "Heave to so that we can come aboard for a search."

"You have no jurisdiction over me," Randell yelled back. "My ship is outside the treaty waters, but you may board if you wish. I have nothing to hide."

The *Wolcott*'s crew lowered a boat for their captain, and he rowed to the Canadian ship while his crew watched nervously as they stood by their guns.

The two captains talked for more than an hour. The *Wolcott* captain tried to strike a deal with the steely eyed Canadian.

"Look, I know you're transporting illegal rum. Hand it over, and I'll let you and your men go free."

The *Wolcott* captain argued that Randell was 10 miles from shore and therefore within his jurisdiction.

"It is within my rights as a U.S. customs officer to arrest you and your crew. I'm giving you a way out."

The American captain gave Randell 15 minutes to make a decision, and he rowed back to the *Wolcott*.

When two hours had passed, the *Wolcott*'s captain shouted, "Have you made a decision yet, Randell?"

"Yes I have," Randell replied. "I'll see you in hell!"

With that, Captain Randell gave the order to flee, and the crew began bringing the schooner around. As the ship slowly pulled away, the *Wolcott* commenced firing. The U.S. cutter fired several shells from her single three-pounder across the *I'm Alone*'s bow. Then, two American crewmen opened fire with wax bullets from Thompson submachine guns. Several shots tore through the ship's rigging and sails.

Young James was terrified. He and the other crewmembers were horrified to see Captain Randell cry out in pain as a wax bullet hit his right thigh.

He reached down and yelled, "I'm okay! Keep her moving!"

Just then, the *Wolcott*'s gun jammed, and she had to stop and call for assistance. Randell kept the *I'm Alone* on a southerly course throughout the night and early morning. He ordered her sails taken down and her engines stopped. The ship was 20 miles off the Mexican coast, and James and the rest of the crew breathed a sigh of relief. They believed they were out of harm's way now that they were close to another country. But their relief didn't last long. Two other Coast Guard cutters had joined the chase when the *Wolcott* radioed for assistance. The *Dexter* and the *Dallas* arrived on the scene about an hour later. They were so close that the American crew could see Captain Randell limping about the deck with his leg in a bandage.

The captain of the *Dexter* ordered the *I'm Alone* to prepare for boarding.

"Heave to, or I shall fire on you."

Randell shook his fist at the Americans. "I'm on the high seas, far from your legal limit. You have no jurisdiction over me."

Both cutters opened fire. Hundreds of shots thundered into the *I'm Alone*, smashing her windows and engines. None of the crew was hit, but she began taking on water.

"Bail boys, bail, or it'll be a watery grave for us all!" Randell bellowed to his terrified crew.

"Heave to, and we'll cease fire!" ordered the Americans. Either Randell ignored the request or pretended he couldn't hear over the din of the gunfire.

Eventually, Randell could see that all was lost. The *I'm Alone* was sinking. He ordered the boats lowered and his crew to abandon ship. The shooting stopped; the once-magnificent vessel silently slipped beneath the waves. The *I'm Alone* was sunk at latitude 25° 45' West by gunfire from the U.S. Coast Guard cutters.

The Coast Guard acted quickly to rescue the men, but one crewmember, Boatswain Leon Mainguy, slipped and fell into the water. He couldn't swim, and he drowned.

The Coast Guard took Randell and crew to New Orleans and jailed them at Customs House. After two weeks, they were released and allowed to return to Canada. The body of Leon Mainguy was shipped home in a pine coffin purchased with contributions from the crew. He was buried in the cemetery near his home in St. Pierre.

Repercussions were heard immediately from Canada, Britain, and France. Even though it was no secret that the *I'm Alone* was a rumrunner, many were outraged over the incident. The initial complaint was the position of the schooner at the point of first contact. Her captain maintained that she was only a seven-knot vessel and that she was anchored about 15 miles out in international waters. U.S. customs disputed those numbers saying that she was 10 miles off the Texas coast, and that it was within their legal rights to open fire. For a year, from March 1928 to April 1929, hardly a day went by that North American and European newspapers didn't carry the story. The violence on the high seas sold many newspapers.

Canada pointed a finger at the United States, accusing the navy of piracy. The Canadian government sent a strongly worded protest to Washington, and the controversy dragged on with years of legal and diplomatic bickering. Finally, the entire incident went before an international arbitration board. Randell was well respected by the Crown for his service record, and his voice was heard when he cried foul about the way the ship went down. It was even suggested that the U.S. Coast Guard should be tried for murder.

The arbitration board decided that the U.S. Coast Guard clearly sank the *I'm Alone* in non-territorial waters, violating the rum-running treaty between the U.S. and Britain. The American Coast Guard's bending of treaty rules to capture the *I'm Alone* seemed more about the captains' egos than enforcing the law. In the end, Canada actually sued the United States over the loss on behalf of Captain Randell and the crew.

In June 1929, in a written statement to the United States government, Canadian Ambassador Vincent Massey filed a lawsuit demanding compensation for the crew members of the *I'm Alone* and their families as well as a formal apology to Canada. It reads:

CLAIM OF THE BRITISH SHIP *I'M ALONE V.*
UNITED STATES
29 Am. J. Int. L. 327
REPORTS OF THE COMMISSIONERS

The I'm Alone, *a British ship of Canadian registry, but de facto owned, controlled and managed by a group of American citizens engaged in smuggling liquor into the United States, was sunk on the high seas in the Gulf of Mexico by a United States Coast Guard patrol boat, with the loss of one member of the* I'm Alone's *crew, on March 22, 1929, after hot pursuit, which began on March 20 within 12 miles of the United States coast.*

Held, that under the Convention of January 23, 1924, between the United States and Great Britain to prevent the smuggling of intoxicating liquors into the United States, the Commissioners could inquire into the beneficial ownership of the I'm Alone, *and that the United States might use necessary and reasonable force to board, search, seize and take the suspected vessel into port; but that the admittedly intentional sinking of the vessel was not justified by anything in the Convention or by any principle of international law.*

Held further, that no compensation ought to be paid in respect of the loss of the ship or cargo, but that the United States ought to apologize to Canada and pay that Government the sum of $25,000 as a material amend, and also pay the additional sum of $26,666.50 for the benefit of the captain and crew of the I'm Alone, none of whom was a party to the illegal conspiracy to smuggle liquor into the United States and sell the same there.

It took several years to untangle the twisted international legal mess. Eventually, the U.S. made a formal apology, and in 1935 agreed to pay $25,000 to Canada as a show of regret for the insult to the Canadian flag and $26,666.50 to the crew. The incident is still used to shape Canadian maritime law today.

In the end, the Canadian Government decided the $26,666 would be divided among Captain Randell and his crew. Two of his sailors had since died, so the money went to their families:

For the captain, John Thomas Randell, the sum of $7,906
For John Williams, deceased, to be paid to his proper representatives, $1,250.50
For Jens Jansen, $1,098
For James Barrett, $1,032
For William Wordsworth, deceased, to be paid to his proper representatives $907
For Eddie Young, $999.50
For Chesley Hobbs, $1,323.50
For Edward Fouchard, $965
For Amanda Mainguy, as compensation in respect of the death of Leon Mainguy, for the benefit of herself and the children of Leon Mainguy (Henriette Mainguy, Jeanne Mainguy and John Mainguy), the sum of $10,185

In submitting this, their final report,
The Commissioners have the honor to be, Excellencies,
Your most humble, obedient servants,
(Signed) Willis Van Devanter
(Signed) Lyman Poore Duff

James Barrett purchased a house in Windsor with his money and decided to find a different job. He'd had enough of the adventurous life of a pirate and decided to find work that would keep him safe and respectable. He married a local girl, got a job on a regular cargo ship and eventually became a well-respected captain himself. He died in 1992 in Bedford, Nova Scotia, leaving behind three grandchildren and two great grandchildren.

Captain Randell became a local hero for his exploits as a rumrunner. He returned home to Halifax, Nova Scotia, where he continued to earn his living as a sea captain on several different ships. He died peacefully in his sleep at his home in 1964 and was given a military funeral.

The highly publicized international affair spawned a popular song about the event written by Canadian folk musician Wade Hemsworth.

And that's how it happened; there isn't much more.
The I'm Alone *became an international affair.*
Skipper John and his seamen were all released
Because the U.S. government couldn't make a case.
That kind of violence is bound to happen
When a law like Prohibition sits up and begs to be broken.
And we still recall
The story of the I'm Alone *and skipper John Randell.*

From song *The Sinking of the* I'm Alone by Wade Hemsworth

CHAPTER SEVEN

The Booze Hounds of Haro Strait
(1920–1933)

"One shot of my whiskey has been known to stop a
man's watch, snap his suspenders and crack his glass
eye all at the same time."

–Roy Olmstead

A STRANGE AND SINISTER PAST haunts the tiny coves, islands and
waterways of southwestern British Columbia. It's no secret in
British Columbia that soon after U.S. Congress passed the Volstead Act in 1919 which led to Prohibition becoming law on
January 1, 1920, rum-running into Washington state from BC
became big business.

On the sea, more than 60 rumrunners operated schooners,
skiffs and trawlers out of the Vancouver area in the 1920s and
early 1930s. Dozens more worked off the west coast of Vancouver Island, Victoria and the Gulf Islands. Vancouver was known
as one of the last few remaining strongholds of smuggled booze
in North America and a rendezvous for rumrunners.

On land, the popular border crossing from British Columbia to Washington state during Prohibition was the Peace Arch
at Blaine. Smugglers often used large, luxury automobiles to

smuggle liquor across the line. Many of these cars had false floorboards covering hiding places that were felt-padded to absorb the sound of clinking bottles. Smiling unsuspecting customs officials waved through well-dressed couples with babies appearing to be on a family outing or a bus full of boisterous school children on a field trip.

As agents caught on to various ploys, the smugglers had to become even more inventive and creative to get their precious cargo into the U.S. They outfitted their cars and trucks with false gas tanks and transported whiskey in bulk. Occasionally, customs agents found the tires of the car filled with booze instead of air!

Without a doubt, Canadian whiskey was a much sought-after commodity south of the border. So much so, many Americans mixed it with their own homebrew to make the illegal liquor last as long as possible.

One of the most colorful and successful rumrunners in the Seattle area at the time was a powerful man named Roy Olmstead. He quickly took advantage of the secrecy and fear that surrounded one island in particular—D'Arcy Island. The American gangster used the island as a hiding place for thousands of cases of bootleg booze.

D'Arcy Island rises out of the fog in Haro Strait about 20 miles southeast of Victoria. The tiny island has an infamous history not only as a favorite hiding place for rumrunners like Olmstead during Prohibition but also as one of Canada's two leper colonies. If the island's rocks could talk, they could tell tales of deceit, piracy and murder.

Olmstead was a big, bald American who worked out of Seattle, Washington. A shrewd and intelligent con artist, the former Seattle police officer had a likable personality with a backslapping good nature and a broad grin that made him a favorite in the community and among his business associates. He was successful because he ran his bootlegging racket

Smuggler Smashup. A bootlegger is killed when he crashes his Stutz Bearcat into a tree at 70 miles an hour during a wild police chase.

like a business rather than a crime syndicate. He liked to brag about the booze he bought from the Canadians to smuggle into the United States.

"Tell ya what," he used to tell his customers, "one shot will curl your hair, and by Gawd, you better be sitting down so you don't have so far to fall."

Rum-running was a lucrative but often dangerous business. Olmstead's Canadian connections bought a bottle for 50 cents in 100-case lots from the Victoria-Phoenix Brewing Company or the Silver Springs Distillery in Victoria, British Columbia. They paid for a shipment in cash, and then the Canadian smugglers quietly sailed out into the harbor under cover of darkness where Olmstead would have one of his many boats waiting to take on the load, buying it for about $2.50 per bottle. Once the booze was transferred from one ship to the other, Olmstead's men would then sail on to D'Arcy Island in the southern Gulf Island chain.

Olmstead had heard about the island's dark history from an old sailor. The island was an almost escape-proof prison for a colony of lepers, established in 1892. Almost all of them were Chinese, and no more than nine people lived on the tiny island at a time. They all lived in meager shacks and were marooned there to die.

Olmstead knew that because of the stigma attached to lepers, the authorities would be hesitant to investigate. He also discovered that the island was not along any shipping lanes, likely because it was located near dangerous reefs. These factors isolated it from other ships and from the prying eyes of the Coast Guard. After weighing the odds, he decided the danger was well worth health and navigational risks to use the island as a stash point for his hooch.

One cloudy night in May 1923, one of Olmstead's captains, Frank Corker, quietly slipped Olmstead's boat the *Eva B* into Haro Strait to pick up a shipment. It was bad weather to be sailing in at midnight, but Frank preferred to smuggle the liquor during foul weather when he was less likely to run into the Coast Guard or hijackers.

Corker had two other Americans with him. One was a tall, thin 22-year-old man named John Chase, who later became the main mob boss for the West Coast Syndicate and eventually spent time at Alcatraz for killing a federal lawman. The other was Howie Sproule, a dim-witted thug hired more for his brawn than his brain.

Frank was a bit of a practical joker, and he didn't bother to tell the hired deckhands that they were heading to a leper colony to pick up a stash of whiskey. He enjoyed scaring the tough goons.

As they rounded the last peninsula that led them into the bay on the southern end of the island, Frank said, "Look smart lads, there's a reception party waiting to greet us."

Four dark shapes stood in the shadows on the pier. As the men strained their eyes and peered into the foggy darkness, they saw that the men on the dock were wearing what looked like long cloaks with hoods covering their faces.

"Ahoy there, we're coming ashore," John called out.

Chase tossed out a line, and one of the hooded men on the dock tied the boat to a post on the pier. As the three Americans got off the boat and stepped onto the dock, they realized that they were suddenly alone. The greeting party seemed to have vanished into thin air.

"C'mon boys," Frank chuckled. "Follow me. I'll show ya where the booze is stashed."

He led his two puzzled deckhands down the dock and up a path through the woods to a small clearing. The men could see a row of shacks constructed from scraps of thin unpainted wood. Unlike Frank, they had no idea that the meager buildings were what the island's residents called home. Smoke issued from two of the stovepipe chimneys, but no one appeared. An eerie silence permeated the night.

Frank pointed to a wooden shed.

"You'll find 823 cases of good Canadian whiskey in there. Haul 'em up on that wagon, and let's get the ship loaded."

The men needed no prodding; they had a bad feeling about the place.

"Hey John, you get the feeling we're being watched?" Howie asked, as he picked up a case and looked around nervously.

"Yup. This is strange. Let's get a move on and get outta here," said John.

They quickly loaded the wagon and pulled the cargo down to the dock. It took six trips to get all the cases out of the shed and onto the ship. As they stepped back aboard the *Eva B*, the four hooded men reappeared out of the darkness. As one mysterious figure untied the boat from it's mooring, another stepped forward and put a foot on the gunwale pushing them off.

John was rolling up the tether rope, when he looked up quickly and caught a glimpse of the face of one of the island residents. He jumped back in horror at the hideously puckered and swollen face under the hood and a quick flash of anguished eyes. His stomach recoiled, and a shiver ran up his spine. He could smell decaying flesh.

Frank chuckled to himself as he motored the *Eva B* in reverse out into the strait.

"Tough boys, all right; scared of their own shadows."

Turning the boat around, he headed out into international waters. In about four hours, they would be at the rendezvous point where another boat would take the cargo off his hands and into Seattle for Mr. Olmstead. The smuggled booze on board the *Eva B* would eventually find its way to a local Washington hotel or neighborhood bootlegger, who then sold it for about $5 a bottle.

Frank, like most rumrunners, had his own selection of ingenious hiding place where he could quickly cache the liquid cargo in case of pursuit. But he didn't have to worry that night. Frank saw that they were all alone in Haro Strait.

Even though rum-running was an inherently hazardous and violent endeavor, Olmstead did not allow his employees to carry firearms. He told his men that he would rather lose a shipment of liquor than a life. Olmstead's men liked working for him, and they were extremely loyal, as were his customers. Within a short time, Olmstead quickly drove his competition out of business with low prices and good-quality booze. He became known as "The King of the Northwest Bootleggers."

With his fleet of boats, warehouses, lawyers and messengers, Olmstead's bootlegging empire soon made him one of the largest employers in the Puget Sound region. Within a matter of months, Olmstead's bootlegging dynasty was generating about $200,000 a month, his legion of loyal smugglers transporting more than 200 cases of Canadian liquor into Seattle daily.

Olmstead's crime spree lasted about six years. The police knew that he was the person responsible for the large quantities of whiskey imported from Canada, but they couldn't prove it. Olmstead's effective smuggling practices made it nearly impossible for the outnumbered Prohibition enforcement agents to catch the bootlegger's ships.

Olmstead's criminal success even forced the U.S. Coast Guard to improve its rusty navy. Bound and determined to catch The King of the Northwest Bootleggers, it added 75-foot "six-bitters" to its fleet. The Coast Guard also converted some confiscated ex-rum-running vessels into government patrol boats. These boats were fast and often heavily armed.

But in the criminal world, all good things eventually come to an end. In 1924, the walls began to tumble down around Roy Olmstead. Surprisingly, however, it wasn't the Coast Guard's new high-powered fleet that spelled the beginning of the end for the Seattle gangster. It was the rapidly evolving electronic technology of the '20s that brought the cocky gangster to his knees.

For months, Prohibition agents had been listening in to Olmstead's calls using wiretaps. In the fall of 1924, they finally decided that they had enough evidence to move on The King. At 2:00 AM on November 26, U.S. federal agents broke down the door of Roy Olmstead's $50,000 home in an exclusive residential area of Seattle. They arrested the bootleg king, still groggy with sleep, and seized five automobiles, a rum-running cigarette boat and more than 240 cases of bootleg liquor at Olmstead's Seattle dock.

But while the defense and prosecution put together their cases and trial dates were set, it was business as usual for the gangster businessman. Olmstead had expanded his stable of Canadian captains who were willing to risk smuggling booze into American waters. Frank Corker introduced Olmstead to a man from Vancouver named Stuart Stone, who became one of Olmstead's most trusted and famous smugglers on the West Coast throughout the '20s.

Captain Stone smuggled liquor from Vancouver south to the western states from 1920 to 1933 on a ship called the *Malahat*. The Reifel family owned the ship, and they'd hired the trusted captain to deliver its liquid cargo. The *Malahat* was a five-masted schooner, built in 1917 at the Cameron Genoa Nulls shipbuilders in Victoria. It had two 160-horsepower Bolinder diesel engines and could carry 40,000 cases in its hold and 20,000 cases on deck.

Olmstead was impressed that Stone had been able to evade the authorities using his cunning, his knowledge of the Gulf Islands, his extensive experience with the shoreline and his favorite hideouts. He hired Stone for $650 a load with a bonus of $100 if the shipment was delivered on time. Stone hired the crew and navigated his ship through Coast Guard-infested waters.

For Stone, smuggling was dangerous work but easy money. He knew the area better than most rumrunners and even most Coast Guard captains, and like Olmstead, Stone used every trick that modern technology had to offer. Coded radio communications from his aunt kept him informed of the Coast Guard's position. She transmitted the warnings from her home above Vancouver's Jericho Beach.

The *Malahat*. This five-masted rum-running schooner could carry a cargo of 40,000 cases of liquor in her hold and 20,000 cases on deck. She was built in 1917 at Cameron Genoa Nulls Shipbuilders in Victoria. The *Malahat* was 245.7 feet long and had two 160-hp Bolinder diesel engines. From 1920 to 1933, Captain Stuart Stone smuggled liquor from Vancouver to the west coast of the United States on the *Malahat*.

She was often pursued and occasionally seized illegally in international waters by the U.S. Coast Guard. After Prohibition the *Malahat* was converted into the world's first self-propelled log barge.

Stone also sailed the *Malahat* to Hawaii for six months at a time where the ship was used as a floating warehouse for fast off-shore craft that ferried booze into island ports. The *Malahat* quickly earned the nickname "Queen of Rum."

On one of his runs to Seattle, Stone met with his boss to discuss the growing problem of hijackers pirating rumrunner's boats, killing the crew and stealing the rum. He wanted to discuss Olmstead's aversion to firearms. They met in the basement of a speakeasy in Seattle's Pike Market neighborhood.

"Roy, I'm going to have to break your rule about carrying guns," Stone said squarely. "Hijacking is getting to be nasty business, and I want some protection. Too many of my friends are getting killed."

"I hear ya, captain," said Olmstead. "I know it's getting dangerous. It's getting so a guy can't even make a good living without worrying about getting shot in the back."

Olmstead not only agreed to let Stone arm himself, he also began making it a practice to put hired gunmen on each of his boats to protect his boys and his precious cargo from pirates. The sailors looked at these hired gunmen suspiciously and with contempt. Their fancy suits and gold and diamond rings seemed out of place on a boat out at sea. But with the increasing bloodshed, the sailors quickly realized these hardened thugs could save their lives.

In addition, the hired guns had a passion for their bloodthirsty business and a flair for the job. Two of Olmstead's hired goons impressed the crew by painting their .45 caliber Thompson submachine guns and pistols gray and trading in their three-piece suits for long gray trench coats, making them nearly invisible while on deck. If would-be hijackers heard that there might be a couple of Al Capone's boys onboard or perhaps one of the deadly shots from Detroit's Purple Gang, they gave the smuggler's ship a wide berth.

In August, Stone sailed the *Malahat* down from Haro Strait, BC, bound for California carrying a load of Canadian whiskey. When Captain Stone docked at Eureka for supplies, a local policeman reported the suspicious-looking craft and crew to federal Prohibition agents. When the ship pulled out the next morning, the Coast Guard cutter *Gaviota*, captained by W.H. Payne, tailed the *Malahat* about 10 miles back.

When the *Malahat* was just a few miles north of Santa Cruz, Captain Payne pulled up closer, grabbed his bullhorn and shouted across the water to Stone.

"This is Captain Payne with the U.S. Coast Guard. I command you to stop and prepare for boarding."

But instead of obeying the order to heave to, Stone gave the go-ahead to head for the nearest cove at top speed. Again, Payne ordered the *Malahat* to stop. When he saw that Stone was not only ignoring his order but also trying to escape, he ordered a shot fired across the *Malahat*'s bow.

Night was falling, and a thick fog was rolling in across the bay. Payne lost sight of the *Malahat*. Disappointed but knowing that it was too dangerous to continue pursuit, Payne called off the search, hoping that the morning light would bring better weather and better results.

Stone slipped into a secluded cove eight miles north of Monterey Bay. He radioed to his contact on shore.

"We've got big trouble. I need to arrange a pickup and fast," said Stone. "It's an emergency, and the sooner we get moving the better."

The contact quickly went to work, arranging to have speedboats go out to the *Malahat* and take the booze safely to shore before morning light. At midnight, the first of the speedboats arrived, and the crews began unloading 40,000 cases of Canadian whiskey. Three gangsters, with their Thompson submachine guns at the ready, stood watch on shore as the job was carried out. Two more hired guns stood watch on the deck of the *Malahat* armed with sawed-off shotguns and Colt .45s.

Once the speedboats with their liquid cargo reached the beach, a line of hired men unloaded the cases fire brigade-style into 13 empty furniture vans. The drivers of these bootleg caravans were nicknamed "land sharks" by both lawmen and gangsters. At about 3:00 AM, the vans pulled out 15 minutes apart to begin the journey to a warehouse in San Francisco.

Now that Captain Stone and his crew on the *Malahat* had their illegal cargo out of the hold and had been paid in full, they could all breathe a little easier. They turned in for the night, planning to slip out of the harbor and sail back north to Canada at dawn. But a different story played out on shore. Things were heating up quickly on the California coast.

Captain Payne had a hunch that Stone would unload his cargo soon after he disappeared into the fog, so he alerted the authorities on shore to keep a watch on Pacific Highway #1 for any suspicious activity over the next 24 hours.

Heeding Payne's warning, U.S. federal agents positioned men along a 50-mile stretch of the coastal highway. At 5:15 AM, the first loaded furniture van rounded the corner at Big Sur. Two agents backed their cars onto the road and forced the van to pull over to the side.

"Get out of the vehicle, put your hands on your head and move away from the truck," one of the feds shouted at the squinty-eyed passenger.

The van driver and his passenger could see that the agent was shaking as he raised his arm and pointed the barrel of his .38 snub-nosed Smith and Wesson at them. Slowly, they opened the van doors, gingerly stepped down onto the gravel roadside and moved away from the truck with their hands on their heads. Agents quickly handcuffed their hands tightly behind their backs and told them to sit down.

"Hey, you can't search our truck without a warrant!" the squinty-eyed driver's helper exclaimed. "That's not legal-like."

"Just watch us," snarled one of the agents.

The agents walked to the back of the truck and untied the canvas flap, revealing case after case of booze piled high. So much liquor was stacked in the back of the truck, the agents marveled that the tires didn't go flat from the sheer weight.

As the agents talked excitedly about the haul, another van came around the corner.

"Quick, let's pull it over," the lawman said, as he drove his car into the road, forcing the five-ton van to a screeching stop. The same scene played out repeatedly as more and more trucks were pulled over; the goons were handcuffed and the cases of liquor were counted.

By 6:10 AM the agents had all 13 vans pulled over and their gangster occupants handcuffed and sitting glumly in paddy wagons. As officers searched the smugglers' papers, they realized they'd hit the jackpot. Among the rumrunners were two notorious thugs, Joe Parente and Frank Cuneo. These tough guys were wanted on a wide variety of charges including attempted murder, kidnapping and rum-running.

A gangster, who was hiding in the back of one of the trucks, jumped off and disappeared into the woods. He was deemed not worth hunting down, but the police fired five or six warning shots, and one of them hit the back of a furniture van. The sound of breaking glass shattered the still night, and whiskey poured out of the truck box and onto the road.

What happened next is one of those strange stories that are passed down from generation to generation because it is such a bizarre tale. Police on the scene later told reporters that the gathering crowd began to press towards the truck. The rubber-neckers could smell the strong, uncut Canadian whiskey as it poured from the truck into the ditch.

"Hey, it's pouring out of the truck like water from a tap," one of the men shouted excitedly.

Before any of the surprised officers could respond, several bystanders took out their handkerchiefs, got down on their knees and began sopping up the liquid. They then began wringing out the booze into their mouths.

One of the officers took out his Smith and Wesson and fired a shot into the air. The crowd broke up at that point, and most ran off down the road. But some refused to budge, and the police were forced to move in and disperse the crowd.

"Better call another paddy wagon, Fred," one of the officers said. "We're taking these hoodlums in with the rest of 'em."

As dawn broke, California police took in 28 gangsters in total. The prisoners were carted off in five paddy wagons and driven to holding cells in downtown San Francisco. The next day, U.S. Commissioner Thomas E. Hayden arraigned them and charged all with violating the Volstead Act and the Tariff Act of 1923. They were released on $20,000 bail each. The 10 arrested for drinking the illegal booze on the roadside were released.

The Big Sur bust was a huge victory for Prohibition agents, but it was a vicious hijacking at sea involving one of Roy Olmstead's smuggling ships that made headlines around the world.

It was early morning on September 17, 1924, when lighthouse keeper Chris Waters saw what looked like a small fishing trawler slowly moving northward up Haro Strait. It looked like the typical 40-foot wooden vessel that was popular among local fishermen. The cabin on these trawlers could sleep four comfortably and had a galley with a four burner propane stove. The boats, known as "fish packers," were often powered by six-cylinder Detroit diesel engines. Chris spotted the boat about three miles east of Oak Bay. At first he thought the fish packer's engine must have broken down, but the boat was too far away for him to see any crew members working on deck. Forty-five minutes later, the craft was drifting out of sight, so Waters rowed out to see if he could catch it or be of assistance.

"Ahoy, there," Waters puffed out of breath as he pulled up alongside. "Anyone aboard?" His only response was the creaking hull and the splashing waves against the side of the *Beryl G*.

With a growing sense of dread, Waters climbed aboard and looked around. He spotted what looked like a pool of dried blood on the deck in front of the cabin door. A wave of panic and fear sent a sickening shiver through his body. His skin went cold and clammy, and he became keenly aware that his heart was beating loud and fast. He couldn't breathe. He slowly backed up to the *Beryl G*'s gunwales and carefully stepped down into his boat with shaking legs. Waters pushed off and quickly rowed back to shore. He ran up the dock and into the marina gas station.

"Hank call the police! There's a boat adrift, and it looks like foul play!" Chris said quietly. "Can you take me back out there with your powerboat so that we can tow her back before she drifts away?"

"Sure no problem," Hank said. "But I think I'll call the cops first."

He called the RCMP and was told that the Coast Guard could have two Mounties on the dock within the hour. Before locking up the station, Hank grabbed his .303 Lee Enfield rifle from behind the closet door. He flipped back the bolt, loaded a shell and put two more in his pocket for good measure. The two took Hank's powerboat and motored out to the *Beryl G*. The wind was picking up, and the boat had drifted even farther north. After about 20 minutes fighting the waves, the two pulled up alongside and hooked up a towline to the boat's bow. They slowly pulled her back to the shore and tied her up at the dock.

The police hadn't arrived yet, so they took a closer look just in case someone onboard was still alive. Chris pointed out the dried blood he'd seen earlier to Hank.

"Hey, take a look at this," Hank said, bending down and running his fingers along the cabin door. "These look like bullet holes to me."

Hank stood up, carefully pushed open the door and peered into the dark cabin. Both men stepped inside and looked around. Furniture, tools and papers were scattered everywhere as if a violent fight had occurred. Waters leaned down and picked up a sea captain's hat that was caked with dried blood.

"I'll bet you my last dollar that this is the work of hijackers. I'll bet this was a rumrunner."

"Ahoy! Anyone on board?" A booming voice shattered the stillness, startling the men. They walked out on the deck.

The Coast Guard cutter was pulling up alongside the *Beryl G*.

"We got your call," one of the Mounties called out through a bullhorn. "Looks like you've made quite a discovery here."

As they came aboard, one of the officials told the men that the *Beryl G* was well known to customs agents as a rum smuggler. As two other officers began to comb the boat for clues, he told Chris and Hank that the boat was registered in Canada and owned by William Gillis of Vancouver. Gillis and his partner, Bert Stechley, were supposedly using the craft to haul cannery supplies, but both men were well known to the Canadian authorities as rumrunners working for The King of the Northwest Bootleggers, Roy Olmstead.

After a thorough search, it appeared that the hijackers had missed some of the booty. The Mounties discovered two cases of Johnny Walker Red hidden under three sacks of potatoes in the hold.

"Hey, look over here!" one of the officers yelled. He came out of the cabin holding a camera containing a partially exposed roll of film.

The police confiscated the boat and told Hank and Chris that the *Beryl G* was now police evidence and that no one was to go onboard. The officers went back to headquarters in Victoria and had the film developed.

Most of the film was overexposed, but one picture was extremely useful to police in their investigation and eventually in cracking the case. It revealed a part of the *Beryl G* and a small powerboat leaving the scene. When police enlarged the photograph, the name on the side of the powerboat was the *Dolphin*.

It didn't take long for police to discover that the *Dolphin* was registered to an American ex-con known as "Cannonball" Baker. Baker, at 39, had spent seven years in McNeil Island Prison for attempted murder in Seattle. When he got out, he joined a San Francisco gang that specialized in running numbers and smuggling booze from Canada. His partner in crime was also a McNeil Island colleague named Harry Sowash.

Sowash was known by American and Canadian authorities for the cleverness of his jobs and for his cruelty. He shot his victims at the slightest provocation, usually beating them unconscious after robbing them. He enjoyed telling the story of how he once set a rumrunner adrift in an open boat in early December because the fellow had hidden money in his shoe.

As captain of the *Beryl G*, Gillis' job was to smuggle liquor from hiding spots such as D'Arcy Island into international waters to various Gulf Island rendezvous points where Cannonball and his crew took over. The last pickup from Gillis had been made on September 15, two days before Chris Waters found the blood-stained *Beryl G* adrift.

BC police interrogated a Victoria fisherman and sometime rumrunner who'd been in and out of jail many times. During the interview, the officers grew suspicious when the man became agitated and refused to answer their questions after they showed him a mug shot of Cannonball Baker.

"Look," said one of the officers to the rattled fisherman, "if you don't come clean and tell us what you know about

Cannonball and the *Beryl G*, we'll send you back to the slammer for withholding information."

He lit a cigarette with a shaky hand and then told the officers a fantastic tale of hijacking and murder at sea. He admitted he'd run into Cannonball picking up supplies at a local marina on Vancouver Island. He said he'd made small talk with the stranger, who told him his name was Norm Hennigar and that he was from Washington State. The men ended up in a local pub where Cannonball bragged about his murderous exploits and told the fisherman in detail how he put his diabolical hijacking plan into action.

"We got real drunk that afternoon," the fisherman said. "This guy you say is Cannonball had a lot of money on him, and he kept buying drinks. When I asked him where he got it, he said that he and his partner, disguised as police officers, hijacked a rum-running boat, killed the crew and stole the booze. I got real scared. He gave me 200 bucks to keep my mouth shut."

The police officers weren't surprised at the incredible tale of murder and deceit. Cannonball Baker had a clean-cut appearance, and he was often known to impersonate law enforcement officers. After a few more questions of the fisherman, and using the photo of the *Dolphin* as evidence, the police solved the mystery of the bloody hijacking of the *Beryl G*.

"Who'd of thought ol' Cannonball would have been so ruthless to carry out such a murderous scheme," one of the officers said, shaking his head at the horror of the crime. "Looks like greed turned him into a wild animal."

Apparently, in August 1924, Cannonball Baker met with a BC police officer in a Seattle apartment. He told the visiting Mountie that he was a U.S. Federal Marshall and that he needed information on rum smugglers for a special Prohibition sting operation. Cannonball asked his Canadian colleague to supply him with whatever data the British Columbia Port

Authorities had regarding the location of liquor caches on the BC side of the border. The well-meaning but naïve officer was only too happy to write out a list of well-known locations.

Cannonball Baker and Sowash chartered a gas boat called the *Dolphin* and headed for Haro Strait. The two goons snooped around the many islands looking for hidden booze but found nothing. They were getting frustrated and angry when another plan began to form in Cannonball Baker's criminal mind.

One afternoon, he and Sowash docked at D'Arcy Island. It had been abandoned for about a year—the last of the lepers dead and buried in a shabby cemetery behind the ruins of their shacks. Cannonball knew it would make a good hideout and a quiet place to formulate his new plan. He and Sowash realized that stealing liquor from the smugglers' caches wasn't going to pay off, so they came up with a more sinister plot to hijack rum-running boats and steal all the booze and money on board.

During an all-night drinking session on the island, they decided it was time for action. Through a fisherman Cannonball had met at a marina, he learned that a boat called the *Beryl G* was making a lot of trips for Roy Olmstead from Canada to Seattle. The fisherman told him that once a month the *Beryl G* would slip out of Victoria harbor and disappear for weeks at a time. That was all Cannonball and Sowash needed to hear.

On September 10, 1924, the *Dolphin* dropped anchor near Discovery Island. Like a spider waiting for a fly, Cannonball waited patiently for his prey to sail into his trap. They didn't have long to wait. At 9:30 PM, the *Beryl G* appeared out of the mist, heading for international waters.

"Here we go Harry. Let's knock 'er off," Cannonball said, quietly.

He swung the *Dolphin* around and quietly motored into the path of the *Beryl G* with lights out. Cannonball fired a flare into the air.

"Stop in the name of the Canadian Coast Guard," Baker called out. "We're coming aboard to search your vessel.

Cannonball Baker and Sowash had blue suits on and were wearing official looking gold-trimmed caps that they'd bought in Victoria. Gillis was not a violent man and figured he'd been caught red-handed by legitimate officials.

As Baker and Sowash came aboard with guns drawn, Gillis and his other three crew members put their hands in the air.

"You got us dead to rights officers," Gillis said. "We're taking a load of whiskey down to Seattle. "You'll find everything in the hold. We always cooperate with the law, so go easy on us."

Baker and Sowash brought out handcuffs and then ordered the *Beryl G*'s crew to turn around.

"Hey, go easy officers. I said we always cooperate with the law. There's no need for this."

Sowash handcuffed the men together and made them lie face down on the deck, the sawed-off shotgun pointed at the back of Gillis' neck.

"Oh yeah, we've hit the mother lode," Sowash cried, as he came out of the hold. "There must be 1400 cases of booze."

All of a sudden Cannonball saw a small figure dart from the cabin and into the hold.

"Well, what have we here," he chuckled, as he reached down and pulled up a nine-year-old boy.

"Hey, hands off my boy," Gillis growled. "That's my son, Nathan. He means you no harm."

Cannonball was holding the boy's arm tightly when Nathan turned and bit the grizzled convict on his wrist, drawing blood.

"Fer chrissakes!" Baker yelled. "I'll teach you!"

He drew back a large fist and hit the boy squarely between the eyes. The boy's small frame slumped to the deck. Cannonball picked him up and threw him into the cabin.

Gillis started crying.

"You've killed my boy," he sobbed.

"That's enough out of you," Baker said, as he kicked the *Beryl G* captain in the ribs.

"C'mon boys, let's get her loaded up."

"What do we do with these guys? They've seen our faces!" Sowash exclaimed.

"Let's turn 'em into fish food. Get loaded up."

Sowash turned his head slightly to the side as he pulled the trigger and blew off the back of the head of one of the crew members. Then turning, he calmly pumped another shell into the chamber and shot the next sailor in the back of the neck and then the last one in the back of the head. Within 30 seconds, three dead sailors lay still on the deck in a growing pool of blood.

Baker pulled Gillis to his feet and marched him across the deck at gunpoint. Gillis sobbed and pleaded for his life, but Baker wasn't listening. He told Gillis to stand in front of the cabin door and turn around. He then opened fire with his Colt .45. He pumped four shots into the captain's back and one into the back of his neck. Gillis slumped to the deck, the cabin door swung open and his blood-soaked hat fell inside.

Cannonball grunted as he pulled Gillis by the leg and rolled his body to the side of the boat beside the other three bodies. Sowash and Cannonball then slit open the bodies with their knives so that the corpses wouldn't resurface and tossed them into the inky ocean depths.

Baker and Sowash transferred the *Beryl G*'s liquor to the *Dolphin* while the two craft, lashed together, headed towards Little Halibut Island. They then cut the anchor free and let the boat drift away; hoping the current would carry it far out into the Pacific Ocean. The winds blew fiercely, and the ocean swelled with six-foot waves.

The sound of the *Dolphin*'s motor awoke Nathan. The quick-thinking boy grabbed his dad's Browning camera, staggered onto the rolling deck and took a picture of the fleeing vessel. His head hurt, and he wandered around the deck trying to figure out what had happened to his dad and the rest of the crew members. The camera then likely fell from his hand and smashed into the hold. It's possible that he then leaned over to try to see where it went, but a fierce swell rocked the boat, and the boy fell overboard. Too weak to swim, he sank below the waves, joining his father and fellow crew members in their underwater grave.

After Stuart Waters and his buddy Hank had hauled the *Beryl G* to shore and the tragic story had been told, the Canadian Coast Guard spent more than a month dragging the area around Discovery Island for the bodies of the crew of the *Beryl G*. But nothing was ever found.

Three months later, after a nation-wide manhunt, Baker was captured in New York City on December 27, 1924. Sowash was nabbed in an unrelated raid of homeless people in New Orleans a month later.

Cannonball Baker and Harry Sowash were brought back to Canada for trial, found guilty of murder and sentenced to death by hanging. It is said that as the hangman tightened the noose around Baker's neck, the condemned man's last words were, "Step on it, buddy. Let's get on with it."

Roy Olmstead went to federal court in January 1926. Evidence showed that he had clearly violated the National Prohibition Act. He was found guilty and sentenced to four years at the McNeil Island Federal Penitentiary and fined $8000. While in jail he converted to the Christian Science faith and began preaching that liquor was destructive to man and society.

When he was released from prison, Roy Olmstead got a job selling furniture. He also started a ministry out of a small office in the Times Square Building in Seattle. Until his death on April 30, 1966, at the age of 79, Roy Olmstead spent a considerable amount of time visiting jails in the Puget Sound area, teaching the bible and trying to rehabilitate prisoners. Franklin D. Roosevelt granted Roy Olmstead a full presidential pardon on December 25, 1935.

When the United States repealed Prohibition in 1933, the era of the Canadian rumrunners along the BC coast was over. The ships that carried thousands of cases of liquor to the U.S. were once again used to haul legitimate cargo for much less money than was made selling contraband Canadian booze to American gangsters. The smugglers went back to earning a living as sailors, longshoremen, fishermen and loggers.

After Prohibition, Captain Stone's ship, the *Malahat* hauled lumber for another decade. Even though the five-masted schooner was beached in 1944 and then sunk in 80 feet of water off the Powell River, 80 miles north of Vancouver, BC, the Queen of the Rum Runners keeps the legends of the Booze Hounds of Haro Strait alive today. From her underwater resting place, The *Malahat* is now a popular site for scuba divers from around the world.

CHAPTER EIGHT

Murder in the Mountains

The Story of Emilio Picariello (1879–1923) and
Florence Lassandra (1901?–1923)

"He is dead, and I'm alive, and that's all there is to it."

–Florence Lassandra

The old woman kneels before the gravestone. The scorching August sun warms the grass in the Fort Macleod, Alberta cemetery. Pearlie carefully brushes aside the dead grass and dirt and pulls out the weeds growing around her father's tombstone. A gentle breeze blows a lock of gray hair across her cheek. Using the headstone for support, the 92-year-old woman slowly pulls herself up pausing to trace her dad's name carved in the marble with her finger—APP Constable Stephen Lawson. Gone but not Forgotten. Born: June 8, 1880. Died: September 21, 1922. Age: 42.

The sleepy little town of Blairmore, Alberta, is nestled in the southwest corner of the province on Highway 3. It was the first town built on the east side of the Crowsnest Pass with the town of Coleman to the west and Frank to the east. But the quiet, unassuming town holds a deep, dark secret from Alberta's Prohibition days. Blairmore is home to one of Alberta's most dramatic murder cases. It reveals a great deal about the ruthlessness that Prohibition triggered in the early days of Wild Rose Country.

Prohibition in Alberta began in 1916 during the term of Alberta's second premier, Arthur Sifton. Sifton's government declared that on July 1st of that year, Alberta would outlaw the casual use of liquor, allowing it for only sacred, medicinal and scientific purposes.

The tough measure was brought about in part because of several political reform movements across the country including the Women's Christian Temperance Movement—a group of women who advocated total abstinence because they were concerned about the problems alcohol was causing their families and society. In addition, many church organizations and moral reformers such as the evangelical William "Bible Bill" Aberhart demanded the complete and immediate eradication of "demon rum."

Prohibitionist hysteria reached a fever pitch in 1916 when Canadian writer and newspaper columnist Nelly McClung began traveling across Canada, the United States and Europe speaking at rallies in support of social change such as Prohibition and women's right to vote. McClung devoted her life to helping women fight for a better world. In her lectures and writings, 46-year-old Nellie preached of the evils of "demon liquor." She said there were too many women being abused by their drunken husbands. She preached that Prohibition was crucial to protecting the rights of women. It was during this time that after a long and well-organized campaign, Alberta became the third province (after Manitoba and Saskatchewan) to grant women the right to vote in provincial elections.

But the outlawing of one of the few pleasures of a hard-working man's life was simply unacceptable to them. When

Prohibition became law, backyard stills began popping up, and the secretive exchange and consumption of spirits became a way of life.

In the 1920s, the Crowsnest Pass looked like the Wild West. Men outnumbered women six to one, and rumrunners and gangsters smuggled hundreds of gallons of illegal booze through the Crowsnest Pass daily. They transported booze from British Columbia, through the Crowsnest into Coleman and Blairmore and down to Montana. Every town had an illegal bar set up in the back of a hotel or a house called a speakeasy or blind pig. These places sold bootleg booze by the glass.

The escalating problems with rum-running and violence kept police officers busy. But it was difficult for the Alberta government to count on hard-drinking, hard-living members of the Royal North-West Mounted Police to throw their hearts and souls into policing the outlaw traffic. So, on March 1, 1917, the RNWMP's provincial duties were terminated, and the Alberta Provincial Police (APP) was formed under Commissioner W.C. Bryan to serve and protect the God-fearing people of Alberta from demon rum smugglers.

It was a thankless job for the 125 officers. The illegal liquor trade was a lucrative business in southern Alberta, and gangsters had a great deal of money to spend on the fastest automobiles and the newest guns. Bootleggers were resourceful and cunning, and some were even regarded as folk heroes by Albertans. As a result, police had a difficult time infiltrating the network of bootleggers, many of whom were protected by hotel owners and others who benefited from the vast amount of money that could be earned in the illegal trade.

When officers realized it was nearly impossible to pursue a smuggler's "souped-up" car with their horses and government-issued vehicles, the Crowsnest and neighboring police detachments outfitted its force with motorcycles and sidecars, equipped with mounted machine guns.

In September 1922, the Crowsnest Pass became one of western Canada's most infamous areas following the brutal killing of a police officer in the town of Coleman. The highly publicized case was instrumental in bringing an end to the eight years of Prohibition in Alberta.

The world was at war in 1917, and a young Italian immigrant was making a name for himself in the Crowsnest Pass as a hotshot, two-bit gangster and whiskey trader. His name was Emilio Picariello, but his friends and family called him "Emperor Pic." He was powerfully built and stocky, standing 5'8" and tipping the scales at 210 pounds. He had piercing brown eyes, dark hair and a black, waxed mustache twirled to fine point. He made friends quickly, and he had a natural flair for business.

Picariello was born in 1879 in Capriglia, Italy. He married Marianino Marucci in 1904, and they had seven children: Stephano "Steve," Angelina Rose "Julie," Carmine, Luigi "Louie," Charles "Chuck," Albert and Florence Eleanor "Helen" (Matson).

The family immigrated to Fernie, BC, in 1911 where Emilio started an ice cream business. He was so successful that at one point he was producing 400 gallons a day. He operated Fernie's first ice cream wagon and opened up ice cream parlors in Blairmore and Trail, BC. He also started his own macaroni factory. In 1918, he bought the Alberta Hotel in Blairmore from Fritz Sick of the Lethbridge Brewing Company.

Under provincial law during Prohibition, a bar owner could produce and sell low-alcohol beer. "Temperance" beer had to have an alcohol content of two percent or less. With Prohibition well underway, Emperor Pic was quick to see a business opportunity waiting to be seized in the brewing and smuggling of liquor into Alberta. The blind pig in his hotel was always filled with customers drinking his low-alcohol booze; it didn't take him long to see the pot of gold at the end of the rum-running rainbow.

Emilio Picariello (1879–1923), bootlegger and wealthy businessman, was also known as "Emperor Pic" and the "Italian
Robin Hood" because of his generosity to the poor.

~⊗~

He went to work setting up a network of stills in the moun-
tains and back-country trails of the Crowsnest Pass with several
friends and business associates. He turned the basement of
the Alberta Hotel into the headquarters of his rum-running
operation and built two tunnels under the establishment—one

ran under the front street, and the other tunnel led to a back alley where the booze could then be loaded and shipped out. Emilio built a strong wooden door, reinforced with iron bars to secure the tunnel under the street, and it was there that the booze was stored.

Liquor was often smuggled into the Alberta Hotel on flour trucks. Drums of illegal liquor were hidden by bags of flour piled high on the outer edges of the truck box. During the night, Emilio and his teenage son Steve hauled the heavy barrels through the tunnel and into the basement. Charles, Luigi, Angeline, Carmine and Helen tapped the barrels and siphoned the liquor into the 40-ounce bottle that Emilio had been collecting for years.

The people of Crowsnest Pass regarded Pic with respect and fondness for his generosity, and he became a bit of a folk hero in the community. He often helped out poor families at Christmas or bought needy children new shoes or tickets to the movies at the Roxy Theater in Blairmore or the Grant Movie House in Coleman. He also often gave away the bags of flour that were used to hide the smuggled booze barrels.

When he made a bid for town council in the early 1920s, he was elected. As his bank account became fatter, he bought $50,000 worth of Victory Bonds to further the war effort. His actions had some townsfolk referring to Emilio as the Robin Hood of Blairmore.

Picariello was also known for his eccentricities. He and his longtime business partner Charles Lassandra caught a bear cub at the town dump one weekend and decided to make a pet out of it. They put a leash on the bear and took it for walks around town, often ending up in Emilio's bar at the Alberta Hotel. The patrons spent hours teaching the bear to stand on its hind legs, begging for peanuts.

The two friends also bought a player piano at a music shop in Calgary and hauled it back to the hotel in Blairmore. Late at night Lassandra's young wife Florence cranked it up and made sure it was playing at full volume to cover up the sounds of the clinking bottles coming from the basement.

Twenty-one-year-old Florence was unhappy in her marriage. Her father had forced her to marry the abusive Charles when she was only 15 years old. She enjoyed the excitement and danger that Emperor Pic offered with his celebrity status as a bootlegging folk hero. And Picariello enjoyed her bold manner and girlish charm. He hired Florence as a chambermaid and nanny to help his wife at the hotel.

She was plain in appearance but always well groomed, wearing her hair and clothing in the fashion of the day just like the silent movie stars she saw on the posters at the Roxy Theater on Main Street. Even though she was no beauty, she could still turn heads when she walked down the street. After all, there weren't many women in the region.

Emilio's handsome teenage son Steven became infatuated with Florence. They weren't far apart in age and had the same taste in movies and music. It wasn't long before the two were in the midst of a passionate affair, meeting secretly late at night in one of the empty rooms in the Alberta Hotel after everyone else had gone to bed.

Emilio suspected that his son was having an affair with his friend's wife. One night about 1:00 AM he heard tiptoeing outside his room in the hall. His son's door creaked open and then quietly shut. He got out of bed and padded down the hallway to room 22. He could hear hushed voices, muffled laughter and then Florence and his son making love in the squeaky, old feather bed. Pic chuckled to himself and quietly returned to his room where his wife Maria was sound asleep. He was secretly proud of his young son's machismo. He had grown into a man.

In the early stages of his bootlegging career, Picariello supplied his thirsty customers by delivering the booze in a fleet of

Florence Lassandra (1901–23) worked for Emilio Picariello as a housekeeper in the Alberta Hotel in Blairmore, Alberta. She was the only woman to be hanged in Alberta.

꧁꧂

Model Ts. He loved the sense of adventure and the thrill of the chase when outrunning the cops. He even outfitted his cars with concrete-filled pipe bumpers so that they could smash through barricades and roadblocks. To the frustration of the police, Emperor Pic and his son Steve managed to slip through every roadblock and trap the authorities set.

Business was good, and as the police beefed up their fleet Emilio, too, began to shop around for faster, more streamlined automobiles. He bought two McLaughlin Six Specials, which were the fastest vehicles on the road in the early '20s. They came straight out of a factory in Oshawa, Ontario, with 50-horsepower six-cylinder engines. So popular were these as liquor-hauling vehicles that they became known as "Whiskey Sixes." Unfortunately, the police only had four-cylinder 22-horsepower engines in their Model Ts and were no match for the mighty "Whiskey Sixes."

Pic sometimes loaded up a car with high-quality booze at the government warehouses in British Columbia and smuggled it into Alberta and then into Montana through a maze of back roads and mountain passes. He'd put the highly-prized 12 per-cent Canadian beer in small barrels. Inside each barrel were three burlap sacks containing 24 quart bottles wrapped in straw. Pic paid about $24 for a barrel of booze, and when he reached the United States, he sold the same barrel for $140. He could carry 14 barrels in his trunk and backseat. One carload of 14 barrels of beer and five cases of whiskey fetched a tidy profit of $2500.

From time to time, Emilio Picariello got caught by police for minor infractions and would have to pay a fine. For example, in the spring of 1921, Sergeant. J.J. Nicholson sent his APP offi-cers to Picariello's hotel.

"We have a search order to go through your liquor barrels in the basement, Mr. Picariello," said Sergeant Nicholson late one night. "There have been rumors that your drinks are stronger than allowed.

Emperor Pic led the Sergeant and two other officers down to the dark basement. Only 13 barrels were stored downstairs that night, and police confiscated every one of them. They took samples from seven of the barrels and sent them off to the lab in Edmonton for testing. The lab found that five of the barrels contained beer that was slightly over the legal limit. The other eight barrels were of legal "temperance" strength. On June 10, Emilio was fined $20. He happily paid the amount and breathed a sigh of relief that his basement warehouse just happened to be empty of the high-test alcohol at the time of the raid.

Emperor Pic must have thought his luck would never run out. He seemed to be able to stay one step ahead of the law on every run he made. One of his regular runs was across the border into Montana to supply American gangsters with Canadian booze. As usual, he packed the beer in burlap sacks, each sack containing 24 quart bottles wrapped in straw to prevent breakage and clinking. South of the border, he met up with an American smuggler named Pat Thomas. Thomas was a tough fast-talking, red-haired bronc rider who was one of the most powerful bootleggers in the Northwestern United States, and he spearheaded one of the most dangerous cartels in the western United States. At one point during Prohibition, he was wanted dead or alive in 47 states. Thomas bought Emilio's entire load for $1250 and then sold it to Al Capone's boys for $2500.

One night, Picariello was returning from Montana where he'd dropped off a load of beer for Thomas and picked up some American bootleg whiskey at a barn near the tiny town of St. Mary, and he was stopped at the border.

"Excuse me sir," the customs agent told the Emperor. "You'll have to get out of the car. We're going to search it."

But Emilio had other ideas. He was carrying eight cases of high-test whiskey in the trunk and over $3000 dollars in cash in a brown paper bag on the backseat with no plans to hand it over. Instead, Picariello stepped on the gas, and the McLaughlin roared to life. In a whirlwind of gravel, dust and exhaust, he made a run for the Canadian side of the border on Highway #6.

The startled customs agent jumped on the Buick's running board and reached in the window to grab the steering wheel.

Emilio grabbed the officer's hand with a vice-like grip and wouldn't let him go until they were well inside Canadian territory. Knowing that he was safe from prosecution, Emilio pulled over and helped the shaking lawman brush the dust off his clothes.

"Sorry about that," Emilio said, "but I'm a Canadian citizen, and there is no way I'm spending time in an American jail. You've only got a two-mile walk back to the border."

Emilio left the customs official in a cloud of dust as he drove through Whiskey Gap and on to Pincher Creek to deliver his precious cargo to his customers.

But Emperor Pic's luck was about to run out. In the fall of 1922, Emilio cut a deal with a wholesale liquor dealer in Calgary to deliver 120 cases of high-grade scotch whiskey. In the past, Emilio only delivered one shipment of 40 cases at a time using one car to slip in and out of town as quietly as possible. But this time, he decided to put together a convoy of rum-runners to get the booze from BC to Calgary in one fast trip. Emilio called a meeting in room 17 of the Alberta Hotel with his son Steve and his mechanic John McAlpine.

"Here's the plan, boys," Picariello said, as he poured each of them a stiff drink. "Steve you'll take one load in the Special, John you'll drive the other and I'll follow in my car. The trick is to drive fast and stay close together. We'll have the load delivered before the cops even know what we're up to."

They toasted each other, lit cigars and agreed that the run would happen in two days, on September 21. The plan was to drive west to Fernie pick up the whiskey and then turn around and head east to Calgary to deliver the load to the wholesaler.

But someone must have talked. A stool pigeon told Sergeant James Scott at Blairmore of Picariello's plan to run illegal liquor from BC to Calgary and that the booze was to be picked up at the government warehouse in Fernie. Scott passed the information on to the APP in Coleman, where Constable

Steve Lawson settled in to wait for the convoy in an abandoned house on Highway #3.

Steve Lawson was born in Brixton, England, on June 8, 1880. He immigrated to Canada in 1903 and joined the Fort Macleod police force in 1907. When war broke out, he enlisted and fought overseas. He was honored for bravery on the battlefield at Vimy Ridge and Passchendaele. On his discharge, he returned to Canada and became Fernie's police chief. In the winter of 1922, he joined the APP and was stationed at Coleman as part of a special unit formed to track and catch rumrunners.

On September 21, a sunny Thursday afternoon, Constable Lawson watched the three-car convoy drive slowly into town. He was surprised by the group's boldness. It was broad daylight, and Emperor Pic and his merry band of smugglers were driving down Main Street. McAlpine was driving the first car; Steve Picariello the second, a McLaughlin Special; and the Emperor brought up the rear. Lawson phoned the detachment in Blairmore to tell them that the rumrunners were on their way. The police knew that Emperor Pic would likely stop at the Alberta Hotel, and that's where they planned to catch him red-handed on his own turf.

Sergeant Scott was the officer in charge of the investigation, and he was on duty in Blairmore that day. He had already prepared for the rumrunners' arrival by getting the paperwork in order so that he could serve a search warrant on the spot when Picariello's team arrived at the Alberta Hotel.

He didn't have long to wait. At about 5:30 PM, the trio drove into town and parked behind the hotel. Sergeant Scott walked up to the men before they were even out of their cars and handed the search warrant to Emilio.

"It's over, Emilio," Scott said. "We've got you dead to rights."

Emperor Pic's eyes went wide, and he sprang into action.

"Run for the hills, boys," he yelled, as he leaned on the Buick's horn. Before the police could jump into their cars, the three rumrunners roared out of town back towards Coleman on Highway #3. The chase was on. The rumrunners drove flat out for the BC border with the police in hot pursuit. But just out of Blairmore, Scott gave up when he realized that his old Model T was no match for Picariello's fast fleet. Returning to the station in Blairmore, he called ahead to Constable Lawson to tell the surprised lawman that the smugglers would likely be making a second appearance in Coleman that day.

When John and Emilio realized that the police had given up the chase, they slowed down and spread out. But Steve was still driving at top speed towards Coleman.

At about 5:40 PM he roared into the tiny town. Constable Lawson was waiting for the young rumrunner. Lawson was standing in the middle of the street, his revolver in his outstretched hand aimed directly at the car coming towards him in a cloud of dust.

At 19, Steve was a skilled and daring driver, thinking himself indestructible as all teenagers do. When Lawson flagged him down, he simply stomped on the foot-feed and gave the "Whiskey Six" all the gas he could. Lawson jumped out of the way and shot twice. One of the bullets hit Steve in his left hand, and the other knocked the bottom rearview mirror off the side of the McLaughlin as it roared by. But instead of stopping, the young smuggler kept driving like a madman east out of Coleman.

Constable Lawson grabbed his Harley-Davidson motorcycle with its sidecar and gave chase. Once again, a wild pursuit was on. But after nine miles, Lawson realized that he'd never catch the speeding smuggler, so he pulled the Harley over, took out his revolver and fired off two shots at the car's fading taillights. He was too late. Steve had disappeared into the cool mountain twilight. Frustrated, Lawson drove the motorcycle back to Coleman where Emilio and John had just arrived. An excited crowd of onlookers gathered around the bootleggers' car.

"Break it up, break it up," Lawson said, as the crowd parted to let him through. Emilio and John were leaning against the McLaughlin smoking cigarettes.

"You might as well go and get your boy and bring him back here," Lawson told Picariello. "The law will go easier on him if he gives himself up instead of me going out to haul him in."

Picariello nodded, quietly got in his car and drove out of town towards the BC border. He believed his son would be waiting for him on the other side. Once he got to the border town of Crowsnest, however, Picariello found out for the first time that his son had been shot.

"Your boy came through here about a half hour ago," a gas station attendant told him. "Looked like he'd been shot in the hand. He stopped and asked me for a bandage."

Pic, not knowing if his son was alive or dead, turned his car around and quickly drove back to Blairmore.

Meanwhile, Steve Picariello had driven himself to Michel, BC. He went to the local hospital where he had his wound treated. His injury didn't appear serious, and he checked out of the hospital, went to police headquarters and turned himself in. He was put in a jail cell for two days when he admitted that he couldn't pay the $100 fine for carrying firearms.

Back in the blind pig at the Alberta Hotel, Emperor Pic was pacing the floor, drinking whiskey and working himself into a rage.

"What's that bastard cop doing shooting at my boy? He could be dead in a ditch somewhere."

Just then the phone rang in the hotel lobby. Mrs. Picariello picked up the receiver.

"All right then," she said quietly and walked back into the bar. Her face was white.

"Steve is in Michel," she told the family. "Someone called to say they saw him in the hospital. He's been shot."

Emilio exploded with anger.

"I swear to the mother of Jesus, if my boy is dead, I'll kill the son of a bitch."

He told his wife to look after the kids and the hotel and that he would be back shortly.

"You're not going without me," Florence stammered. She'd been sitting in one of the lobby chairs listening. "I have to know if Steve is alive or dead."

Emilio told her to get in the car parked out front. He opened the office door in the lobby, walked over to the closet and took out two handguns and a box of shells. He loaded the pistols as he walked out the front door and slid into the driver's seat of the McLaughlin. He gave Florence a .32-calibre Colt autoloader. He tucked a .38 Smith and Wesson under the car seat, and together they roared off to make the five-mile journey to Coleman as quickly as possible.

They arrived in front of Constable Lawson's barracks about 7:00 PM. Lawson's home was his office and residence. The police officer, his wife and five children—Pearlie, Mary, Steve, Peggy and Kathleen—had finished supper about 15 minutes earlier. Lawson was fixing an axe handle, and the children were playing in the living room. When he heard the commotion outside as Emilio drove up, Lawson walked out the front door to the car wearing only his undershirt, pants and boots. He was unarmed. He rested his foot on Picariello's running board on the driver's side and leaned in the window.

Picariello grabbed the astonished officer by his shirt and hissed, "You shot my boy, and you're going with me to get him."

"Oh yeah, what about it?" said Lawson. "I have no idea where your rum-running, no-good son is."

The two men struggled. When Picariello reached down with his other hand to try to grab the pistol Lawson reached in and grabbed Emilio by the neck. During the fight, two shots rang out. One bullet smashed through the speedometer. The other pierced the rubber molding at the bottom of the front windshield. Lawson broke away and ran towards the southwest corner of his house. Two more shots rang out. One bullet missed him, but the other tore into the constable's right shoulder blade and came out the left side of his chest. Blood poured from the wound, as the APP officer fell face-down in the dirt at the side of the road.

Tires spinning in the gravel, Emperor Pic tromped on the gas pedal and hurdled away from the scene. Lawson's wife and her daughter Pearlie ran screaming out of the house to their fallen husband and father lying in the dusty, blood-soaked street.

Two young boys who'd heard the shooting paused to look at the fallen officer and then ran to the doctor's office beside the Grant Theater. Another APP officer, Constable Day, ran to Lawson, but it was too late. Lawson was dead, blood streaming from his mouth. As Day knelt beside Lawson, he turned and asked little Pearlie what she saw.

"Daddy fell down, and a man in a big car drove away," the shaken youngster said. "The woman beside him wore a red hat and a blue coat."

The entire incident had taken only about six minutes.

Emilio Picariello and Florence Lassandra drove the five miles back to Blairmore in silence. He parked the car north of the Cosmopolitan Hotel in Blairmore and told Florence to walk across the tracks and hide out in his bartender's home. Emilio snuck through Blairmore's back alleys to his hotel and in the back door. He sat down at the kitchen table, and in a shaky voice, told his wife Marianino what had happened.

Constable Stephen Lawson (1880–1922) was a well-respected member of the Alberta Provincial Police (APP). He'd been with the force for only six months when he was gunned down outside his family home and police barracks in Coleman, Alberta, on September 21, 1922. Before becoming a police officer, Lawson fought in WWI with the Fort Garry Horse. He received a medal for meritorious service and his heroic actions on the battlefield overseas. The 42-year-old was a veteran police officer who had worked in law enforcement for more than 10 years, most notably as the chief of police in both Fort Macleod, Alberta, and Fernie, British Columbia. When he transferred to the Alberta Provincial Police in March 1922, Lawson was assigned to D Division which extended from Lethbridge east to the Saskatchewan border, west to BC and south to the U.S. border.

"I just want you to know that I'm innocent. I never killed no cop. It was Flo who shot him."

He had a couple of quick shots of whiskey and kissed his wife goodbye.

"I've got to go hide out until this all blows over. I'll be back soon."

He drove his McLaughlin Six slowly out of town and disappeared into the mountain night, heading north on an old coal mining road.

The next morning, Friday, September 22, 75 police officers began scouring the foothills with tracking dogs looking for the runaway rumrunner. They believed the wealthy bootlegger was hiding with friends somewhere between Coleman and Fernie. The posse was determined to get their cop killer dead or alive.

Little did the lawmen know that the stocky Italian had driven back to the Alberta Hotel under cover of darkness, hidden the car and was sitting in his blind pig waiting to be arrested. He'd come up with a plan that he believed would keep him out of jail.

That Friday evening, APP Sergeant Scott walked into the front lobby of the Alberta Hotel to question Mrs. Picariello. He was stunned for a moment to see Pic sitting by the player piano with a tall glass of whiskey in his hand and smoking a big cigar.

"You're under arrest," Scott stammered, reaching for his gun, "for the murder of Constable Stephen Lawson."

"I know, I know," Pic said. "No need for handcuffs; I'll come along peacefully. I never killed nobody in my life."

"Where's Lassandra?" Scott asked.

Pic pointed across the railroad tracks.

"She's at Castangi's house."

Scott took Emilio to the police station, booked him and put him in a cell. Then he went to find Florence.

True to Pic's word, she was at Castangi's house sitting on the back porch.

Scott walked up to her, and before he could say a word, Florence said, "He is dead, and I'm alive, and that's all there is to it."

"You'd better come with me," Scott said.

"I don't want to be any trouble, sir," the young woman said. "You'll find the gun is at Mrs. Gibeault's house in a jacket pocket in the closet."

Emperor Pic had already decided that he was going to put the entire blame for the killing on Florence. He firmly believed the Alberta justice system would never hang a woman. He'd told the naïve young woman as they drove back from the murder scene Thursday night that she should take the blame for the killing. After all, he was a wealthy man, and he promised to hire the best lawyers around to clear her name.

Under heavy police guard, Picariello was taken to the Lethbridge jail to await trial. Florence Lassandra was taken to a women's jail in Calgary.

On October 2, the opera house in Coleman was packed for the preliminary hearing. Twenty-eight witnesses were called in for examination. At the hearing, in front of hundreds of onlookers, Pic looked pale and nervous. When Steven Lawson's wife appeared in the courtroom, his eyes filled with tears. Florence, on the other hand, appeared relaxed and at times even cheerful, smiling occasionally at the throng of onlookers. She was smartly dressed in red, with silk stockings and expensive shoes. She chewed gum constantly.

She waved to her girlfriends as court adjourned saying, "Friends, I'll be with you again."

While awaiting trial in his cell in the Provincial Gaol in Lethbridge, Picariello wrote home to his wife in Blairmore. Steve was back home with his family, and Emilio stressed his concerns over his son's medical care. Steve's gunshot wound was infected, and Emilio was concerned that Steve wasn't getting proper treatment.

> *October 29, 1922*
> *Mrs. Picariello*
> *Blairmore, AB*
> *Box 10*
> *Dear wife and family;*
> *I just write this these few lines to tell you if our boy Steve does not get any better I want you to take him to Coleman Hospital. He will be better taken care of there and do so at once if it is necessary. I do not want you to get our local Doctor. I don't like him. He is a phony. Dear wife, write soon and how's the other kids and Angiolina? I received a letter from our boy Carmine. Write me soon Charlie. Mr. Gillis came up Saturday and everything is going good. Give my best regards to our friend, also Florence, give my best love and kisses to our children.*
> *Your loving husband and father*
> *E. Picariello*

By modern standards, it was a speedy trial. Albertans watched with fascination as the circumstances of the murder of Alberta Provincial Police Constable Stephen Lawson unfolded.

Alex A. McGillivray led the prosecution, and John McKinley Cameron stood for the defense. Cameron was well-known across Alberta for his razor-sharp mind and clever courtroom skills. Presiding over the entire procedure was Supreme Court Justice William L. Walsh, who nine years later became the third lieutenant-governor of Alberta.

Also appearing in the Supreme Court chambers in Calgary in November 1922 was the attorney general of Alberta, John. E. Brownlee. That Brownlee himself was present to lay

William L. Walsh (1857–1938), the judge at the murder trial of Emilio Picariello and Florence Lassandra; Alberta's lieutenant-governor from 1931 to 1936

the murder charges and subsequently remained for the full five days of the trial was unprecedented in Alberta's history. Lawson's murder was the third police murder in connection with bootlegging, and the public and the legal system wanted quick justice.

As the trial proceeded, the crowd and the legal experts heard more than 30 witnesses testify about the details of the crime and the circumstances surrounding the events. Ears strained outside chamber doors, and on several occasions, Justice Walsh ordered the noisy corridors cleared.

At no time in the proceedings did either Picariello or Lassandra take the stand, and even as Justice Walsh prepared to hand down the sentence, the accused declined to make statements, remaining silent, exhausted and visibly distraught as Justice Walsh decided their fate.

On December 2 at 8:00 PM, the jury delivered its verdict: "We find both of the accused, Emilio Picariello and Florence Lassandra, guilty of murder," declared the foreman.

Picariello appeared sullen and emotionless. Lassandra, held steady by her matron, appeared on the verge of collapse. The crowded courtroom went silent as the audience leaned forward to hear the judge.

Judge Walsh said, "I concur with your verdict of conviction. Mr. Picariello, please rise."

Emilio's dark eyes were fixed on the judge.

"Under British law, there is only one sentence that can be handed down to a murderer; that is death. You will be taken to Fort Saskatchewan Jail where you will remain until February 22, when you will be taken from your place of confinement and hanged until dead. And may God have mercy on your soul."

Pic slumped back into his chair and stared unblinking at the judge. He didn't hear a word as Lassandra was sentenced to the same fate. Florence moaned as she too sank back into her chair. Her matron steadied her with a hand on her arm.

Emilio and Florence were taken by train to Fort Saskatchewan Jail and incarcerated on death row. The tiny cells were a shock to the condemned inmates. Each cell had a bed, three thin blankets, a toilet and a metal tray table that flipped out of the wall. There was no chair.

Cameron appealed the guilty verdict based on 33 points, which suspended the date of execution to May 2 pending the decision of the Alberta Court of Appeal. But the outcome was not what the defense had hoped for. The decision was four to one in favor of the original verdict.

A second appeal, as well as a plea from the Canadian Prisoners' Welfare Association to Prime Minister William Lyon Mackenzie King for final clemency for Lassandra, were also unsuccessful.

It was one of John McKinley Cameron's most famous defense cases, but one of his bitterest defeats. In later years, he would often say that he never thought that Picariello and Lassandra were the ones who killed Constable Stephen Lawson. He believed that another gunman nearby fired the fatal shot.

From his jail cell on April 27, Picariello wrote a brief note to his wife:

> *Appeal is dismissed, but there is still hope. Best love and kisses to you and all the children.*
> *Your loving husband*
> *E. Picariello*

On the evening of May 1, Florence was in a terribly agitated state and appeared on the verge of going into shock. She paced back and forth in her cell. The prison chaplain, Father Fidelis, was called, and he stayed with Florence most of the night. Fidelis was a Franciscan friar at the little Roman Catholic Church near the prison gates.

Florence asked the priest to order her a bouquet of tiger lilies to be brought to her cell the night before her execution so she could carry them to the gallows. They never arrived. She also ordered her last meal—scrambled eggs, white toast and tea.

Emilio spent the evening before his execution alone in his cell writing this letter to his wife:

Tuesday, May 1, 1923
Mrs. Picariello
Blairmore, Alberta
Box M
My dear wife and children. I expect this will be the last letter I will be able to write to you and the children. I go to the scaffold tomorrow morning an innocent man, and I am prepared to meet my maker. I hope that you and the children will live good and happy lives together and that we will all meet again. According to the will you have from me you are the sole executors until Steve our son becomes of age and then you will both become trustees. And I wish that they all get an equal share. I want you to know that I do not owe anybody. I want you to know that Mr. E. Gillis (lawyer) has already had $4500 from me and I consider I overpaid him for work he had never done. All other lawyers are paid in full. I want you to know Steve I did not authorize Doctor Oliver to attend anybody professionally outside of our own family. I want you to remember all the people I have helped at different times. They have forgotten me now and don't come to help or cheer me. I will say goodbye with love to you all children till we all meet again and may God bless and keep you all safe. Kiss all the children for me.
   Your loving husband and father
   Emilio Picariello
   Fort Saskatchewan Gaol

At 4:30 AM on Wednesday May 2, 1923, the condemned man ate his last meal—a hearty breakfast of sausages, eggs and black coffee. He seemed to enjoy every bite. After breakfast, the prison guards gave Emilio two ounces of whiskey but no morphine. The narcotic was given only to condemned women prisoners. He shot the whiskey back in a single gulp.

At 5:00 AM, Picariello was taken out of his cell and led to the gallows in shackles and chains. He didn't say a word. Warden Driggs led the death procession, followed by two guards flanking Picariello. Father Fidelis was behind Emilio, reciting the prayers for the dying.

Florence was wide awake in her cell when the prison matron brought her breakfast. She didn't touch her last meal. Around 4:45 AM the prison doctor arrived and gave her a shot of morphine along with two ounces of whiskey.

At 5:10 AM Emilio entered the hanging room. The scaffold loomed in front of him, rising 12 feet high. The noose was attached to an iron hook in the ceiling. Picariello walked unassisted up the 18 steps that led to the gallows platform. He positioned himself squarely on the trap door and looked down at the circle of people below him—12 people, including the executioner, the warden and Father Fidelis.

The executioner bound the condemned man's arms to his sides with leather straps and lashed his ankles together.

When Emilio saw the black hood, he turned to Father Fidelis and said, "Please Father don't let them cover my eyes! Please don't let them cover my eyes."

The warden shook his head. It was the law to cover the face of a condemned person. The executioner stepped forward and placed the hood over Emilio's head. He then placed the noose over Pic's head and secured the knot behind his left ear. Witnesses could see Emilio breathing heavily beneath the black bag.

"Have you anything to say?" asked the warden.

"You're hanging an innocent man," whispered Pic. "God help me."

The executioner reached forward and pulled the trap door lever. Emperor Pic dropped into eternity at exactly 5:15 AM.

His body was cut from the ropes, and at 5:25 Dr. R.B. Mooney, the prison physician, pronounced him dead. Emilio's neck was broken. His body was placed in a pine coffin in the hallway outside the hanging room. Beside it was a second coffin—empty—the lid propped up against the wall.

Two minutes later, a pale and shaken Florence Lassandra was led onto the scaffold. The executioner bound her arms and feet with the leather straps. When Father Fidelis began to pray, Florence cleared her throat and interrupted him.

In a trembling whisper, she said, "I have never done harm to anybody in this world. Pic, he lied and lied and lied."

"Have you anything further to say, Mrs. Lassandra?" the warden asked.

"I forgive you all!" she said in a strong voice.

Those were the last words Florence Lassandra ever spoke. The trap door opened, and she fell to her death at 5:51 AM. Eleven minutes later, Dr. Mooney pronounced her dead, and her body was placed in the other coffin. The faces on all those present were ashen. No one spoke as the hanging room was cleared.

Neither Emilio's family nor Florence's husband ever claimed the bodies. Florence's husband, Charles, had disowned his unfaithful bride even before the trial began. The two were buried in unmarked graves in a Roman Catholic cemetery in north Edmonton. To this day, Florence Lassandra remains the only woman to be legally hanged in Alberta and only the fifth woman to be hanged since Confederation.

A year later, on May 10, 1924, Prohibition came to an end in Alberta. The era of rum-running and bootlegging faded into the history books.

In the late '30s, while a Blairmore work crew was repairing a sidewalk, they discovered a large cache of well-aged whiskey in a deep pit lined with railroad ties. Workers dragged out more than 80 burlap sacks filled with bottles. At the bottom of the musty pit, they found a rotting trap door and a tunnel. It led to the basement of the Alberta Hotel.

Once, during Prohibition, I was forced to live
for days on nothing but food and water.

–W. C. Fields (1879–1946), American Actor

NOTES ON SOURCES

The dialogue in this book is true to the sources, and the accounts described are fictionalized as little as possible.

Author Unknown. "Rum Row." The Montreal Gazette, December 11, 1923.

Burroughs, William. *The Last Words Of Dutch Schultz*. London: Cape Golliard Press. 1970.

Burton B. Turkus and Sid Feder. *Murder, Inc: The Story Of The Syndicate* . London: Perseus Books Group, 2003.

Hennigar, Ted. *The Rum Running Years*. Hansport, NS: Lancelot Press, 1981.

Hunt, C.W. *Booze, Boats and Billions: Smuggling Liquid Gold*. Belleville, ON: Bella Flint Publications, 2000.

Marrus, Michael R. *Sam Bronfman: The Life And Times Of Seagram's Mr. Sam*. Waltham, MA: Brandeis University, 1991.

Mill, Eric. *Chesapeake Rumrunners of the Roaring Twenties*. Centerville, MD: Tidewater Publishers, 2000.

Morton, James. *Gangland International: The Mafia And Other Mobs*. New York: Little Brown And Company, 1998.

Turkus, Burton B. and Sid Feder. *Murder, Inc: The Story Of The Syndicate* London: Perseus Books Group, 2003.

Waters, Harold. *Smugglers Of Spirits: Prohibition And The Coast Guard Patrol*. Fern Park, FL: Hastings House, 1971.